A New York Press Photographer's Story

By Tom Middlemiss
Copyright © Tom Middlemiss 2021

tom@eventpixer.com

www.eventpixer.com

All rights reserved, including the right to reproduce this book, or portions thereof, in any form. No part of this book may be reproduced, downloaded, transmitted, reverse engineered, decompiled or stored in or introduced into any storage or retrieval system in any form or by any means, electric or mechanical, without the express written permission of the author.

Except for the public domain photo of the antique wooden phone, all the photos in the book were taken by Daily News Photographer Tom Middlemiss while in the employ of that paper, which has generously given permission for their use.

Dedicated to my wife Marianne, daughters Elizabeth and Kathleen, as well as all the police officers, firefighters and first responders. God bless them for all they do.

"Yesterday is gone.
Tomorrow has not yet come.
We have only today. Let us begin."
(Mother Teresa)

NEW YORK'S PICTURE NEWSPAPER

At the end of World War II, there were 11 widely read newspapers in the New York metropolitan area. Today, only four major dailies remain: *The New York Times, The Wall Street Journal, The New York Post* and the *New York Daily News*. Of those, the latter two are tabloids and could be considered "local" papers.

The *Daily News*, as it is officially titled, was founded in 1919 and is currently the ninth-most widely circulated daily newspaper in the United States.

Known for its bold photographs and often-irreverent headlines, the slogan of the *Daily News* from 1920 to 1991 was "New York's Picture Newspaper", and a camera is still part of the newspaper's logo. Other publicity campaigns have described the paper as "New York's Hometown Newspaper" and "The Eyes, the Ears, the Honest Voice of New York". The *Daily News* continues to prominently display large photographs, for news, entertainment, and sports.

In 1928, a *News* reporter strapped a small camera to his leg, and shot a photo of Ruth Snyder being executed in the electric chair. The next day's headline: "DEAD!". In 1975, after President Gerald Ford refused to help New York City avoid bankruptcy, the next day's front-page headline: "FORD TO CITY: DROP DEAD". Ford later said the headline cost his reelection.

New York City's Police and Fire Departments had great respect for Daily News photographers and reporters, and the feeling was mutual. One reason was the "Hero of the Month Award", which was presented to a police officer or fireman who went beyond the performance of his/her normal duties. It included a check for $250, given to the hero's spouse. And, of course, a photo in the paper with the respective Commissioner. It was a wonderful way to promote great relations with the uniformed services of the Big Apple.

From 1960 to 1982, staff photographer Tom Middlemiss took thousands of photos for his beloved newspaper, many of which are reproduced in this book. You will see photos that will be graphic and horrifying to some readers. And others that will show warmth and compassion.

Middlemiss now lives in Naples, FL with his wife, Marianne.

MY CALLING

It all began at the age of nine, when a friend of the family gave me a Brownie Reflex camera she had purchased from a store in Brooklyn.

I was hooked.

Following in my brother's footsteps, I began taking pictures and developing film in my parent's basement, hanging the 620-mm film on clothes pins on a string all over the room. The smell of developer and hypo permeated the whole house and I loved it. (Mom was not so keen about it.)

Growing up. I had a lot of odd jobs. I even worked in a pawnshop. But I always knew I would someday make a career out of photography.

I had served six months of active-duty infantry training in the United States Army Reserve at Ft. Dix, N.J., when a neighbor, who was a paper handler at the Daily News, suggested I apply for a position as a copy boy at the famed tabloid. I was accepted, and earned the magnificent sum of $48.00 per week in 1960.

My initial duties included taking copy from one desk to an editor when a re-write man yelled "COPY!", and getting lunch for supervisors. The best part of the job was accompanying staff photographers to the racetrack, a baseball game or some other plum assignment, bringing back the film to be processed in the lab.

The Daily News used lots of accident, shooting and fire photos, many of which were in the early morning hours when only two staff photographers were on duty for the whole city. This was something I knew I could tap into to earn extra money, so I purchased a 4x5 Speed Graphic camera at a pawnshop. Film was no problem. I could always get what I needed from the staff "photogs". I also bought two WWII tank radios at an Army-Navy surplus store on Canal Street in Manhattan, which allowed me to tune into the New York City Police and Fire Department frequencies.

I placed the radios on either side of my bed: one tuned to the Brooklyn North frequency and the other to Queens, as I lived on the border of both New York City Counties, and could reach "good" calls in record time in the light-traffic wee hours. This gave me great exposure, and I learned what it took to become a good Spot News photog. I also doubled my weekly salary.

One such call came over the Brooklyn police radio at 3:45am on July 19, 1960. A cab driver had been stabbed to death in the Bedford-Stuyvesant section of the borough. I raced to the scene at Greene and Nostrand Avenues, where I was let into the crime scene by a police officer who pointed to the taxicab. I aimed my Speed Graphic at the open front right door of the Checker cab and hit the shutter button. The #40 flashbulb lit up the scene as if it were daylight, showing the driver, identified as Irving Davis, 40 years old, lying dead sprawled across the front seat, with blood from a severed artery pooling on the street.

It was a gruesome sight, but one which the Daily News was eager to print, especially since I was the only photographer to cover the murder. The headline above the story read, "That Dreaded Voice In The Rear And Another Cabbie Is Dead." (Detectives arrested a man for the crime, who was sentenced to prison for the murder).

This was the first photo I had published in the Daily News and earned me $25, more than half of my weekly salary.

Many of the photos in this book may also be disturbing. But many will show the best of New York City.

And all will depict life as it was in the Big Apple from the 1960s to the 1980s.

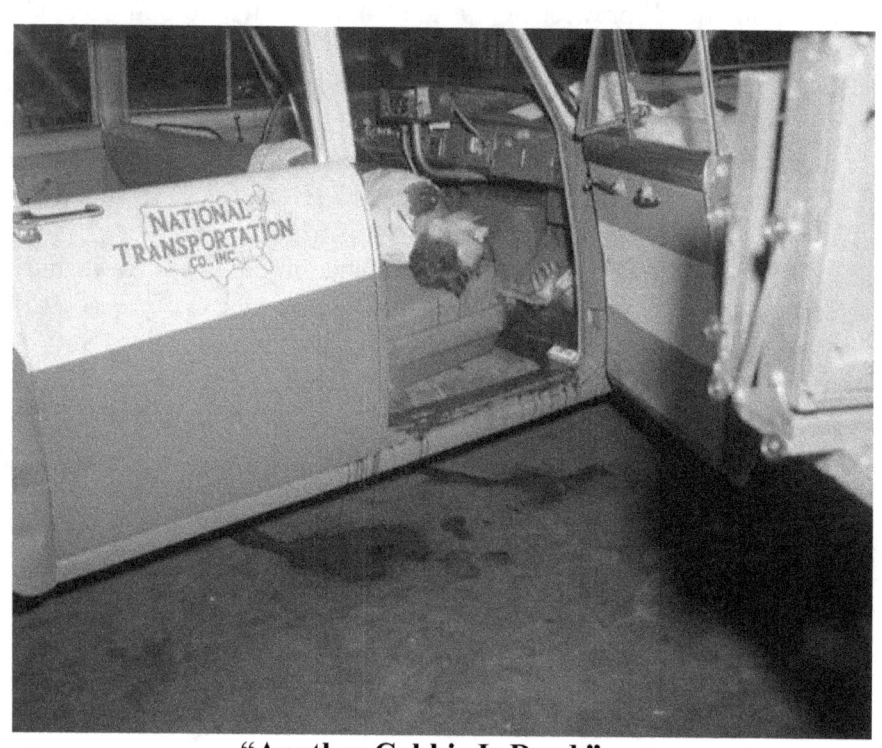

"Another Cabbie Is Dead."

MOVING UP

After a year as a Copy Boy, I was promoted to Studio Apprentice. This was a dream come true, for it meant that eventually I would become a Staff Photographer for the largest circulation newspaper in the United States. There was one hitch. An apprentice had to wait for a staff photog to retire or die. I was number eight in line.

Apprentices developed film, washed and dried prints, and wrote captions for those photogs who worked in the field and hardly ever reported to the main office in midtown Manhattan. When work had to be done, it was all hands-on deck. But there was down time, when we could relax until the next assignment arrived. We had fun. Mischief was always in the works.

Barring a catastrophe, Sundays were particularly slow, with a Yankee or Mets baseball game being the main assignment. Once, five of us got together for a game of nickel-and-dime poker in an unoccupied printers' room. You could have cut the cigarette smoke in there with a knife.

The sliding door opened and Al Pucci, a supervisor, told us there was work to be done. We jumped up, completed the task and, of course, found another print room to get the game going again. This, after he told me there was to be no playing stud.

Well, this print room sliding door opened, and there was Al, again saying that there was more work to be done, which we did, in record time. Al also reminded me that he told me that there no playing stud. \

My answer, "We were playing five-card draw Al." We never played poker again.

Another incident that brings back frat-house memories: When a photographer passed away, a supervisor asked an apprentice to empty the deceased's locker. The idea was to give the contents to him, making sure nothing inappropriate was given to the widow. One fellow found an ancient spread pan, and the powder used with it. This was the gadget photogs used for lighting in the old days before flash bulbs came into existence. He proceeded to roam through the studio setting off the spread pan, which not only gave out tremendous light, but smoke that caused the studio, as well as the entire city room full of reporters and rewrite men, to clear out.

The Fire Department even arrived!

Another hilarious incident occurred when a not so popular supervisor threatened to suspend an apprentice for some photos that happened to have the corners cut off. That was a big mistake to make to a group of twenty-year-olds feeling their oats. The supervisor's mail was snipped, as well as his calendars and all his mounted photographs that were on display in the studio. Some of them even wound up being pasted on the ceiling.

The captain of the Daily News Guards came into the studio and requested that we stop screwing around with the supervisor's photos, because "he wants me to post a guard here all night." The shenanigans ceased; we all loved Captain Jack.

Of course, it wasn't all fun and games.

Around 2am on January 19, 1961, frantic calls came over the Queens police radio: "10:13" (officer needs assistance, shots fired); "10:30" (holdup); "10:20" (ambulance responding).

It doesn't get more important than that: An officer was involved in a shooting, and someone was injured. I sped to the address, a tavern some 10 miles from my home on the Queens-Nassau County border. There, I found off-duty police officer Jack Gally speaking with police captain Simon Vertun about the shooting.

Gally had been seated at the end of the bar when two men with drawn guns walked in and announced a holdup. He took his weapon out its holster, keeping it next to his leg. When the holdup man, later identified as Edward Haughie, approached him and demanded money, the quick-thinking officer spun the bandit around and shot him. The wounded thug's partner, Thomas Caramello, fired six shots at the brave cop. Gally didn't flinch. He fired five times at

Caramello who fled out the front door. He was found dead in a bakery store entrance some two blocks away. Gally hit him five times.

I took photos of the dead bandit, as well as the hero cop speaking with Captain Vertun. Both shots were used in the paper the next day.

In fact, they made Page 1!

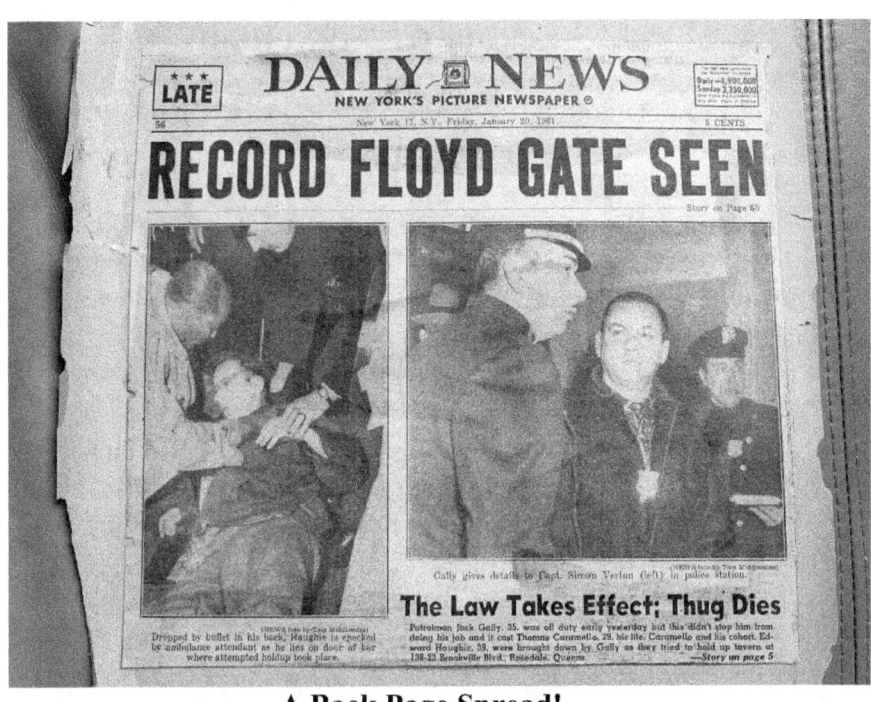

A Back Page Spread!

STAFF PHOTOGRAPHER!

I was promoted to Staff Photographer in 1964. The main office was located at 220 East 42nd Street in midtown Manhattan. From 1929 to 1995, the Daily News was based in that landmark skyscraper near Second Avenue. (The building lobby was the model for the fictional Daily Planet in the first two Superman films.) The paper also had offices in Queens, Brooklyn, the Bronx, lower Manhattan, and New Jersey. I worked in the main office for a while, and then was transferred to Brooklyn to work with Nick Sorrentino, Leroy Jacob, Chuck Frattini, and a reporter, Joe Kiernan. My new digs lacked any semblance of glamour. We referred to as the "shack". There was a greasy-spoon on first floor, and the smell of food they cooked permeated the whole second floor. But we all thought it was a fun place to be.

The shack was located directly across the street from the front door of the "seven eight" Precinct, which was Brooklyn Police Headquarters. It was located at 65 Sixth Avenue and Bergen Street, but was always known as the "Bergen Street Station House". The "seven eight" was a beehive, where people arrested the night before were photographed and fingerprinted. We also had a direct telephone line to the lieutenant in charge of communications for the whole borough. The phone was right out of a 1920's movie, with an exposed bell and a crank. When it rang, you knew something newsworthy was happening.

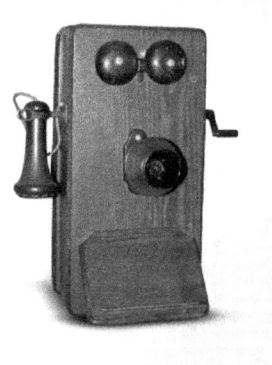

HEART WRENCHING

It was about 3am on Easter Sunday morning when a call came over my Brooklyn fire radio about an "All Hands Operating" at a four-story tenement at 853 Marcy Avenue in the Bedford Stuyvesant section in the Borough.

I raced to the scene and found it hard to describe. The street in front of the building had at least four fire trucks with firemen stretching hoses and pouring water onto the structure.

A minute after I arrived, a woman ran to the firemen screaming that her babies were in the building. Acting on instinct, the tot finders raced into the inferno, searching for the children. Their efforts were in vain, as three children perished.

Fireman George Goldbock and Brian Preston never gave up. They tried in vain to save Eric Peterson, 18 months old by mouth-to-mouth resuscitation.

The photo I made showed the firemen doing their best to revive the infant, his little legs burned and arm hanging motionless. It was heart wrenching.

The Newspaper Guild of New York named it the Best Spot News Photo of 1964. To this day, I wish they could have saved little Eric.

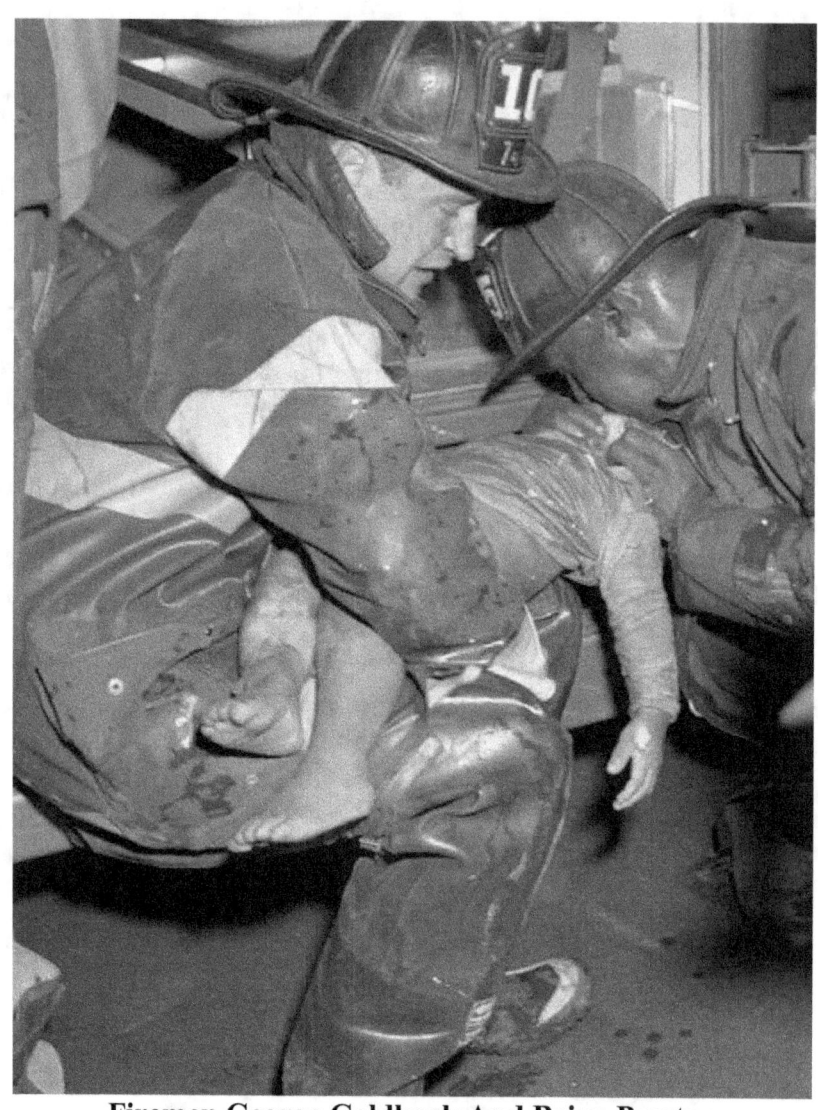

Firemen George Goldbock And Brian Preston Try In Vain To Save Toddler Eric Peterson.

THE RIGHT KIND OF FRIENDS

I had two friends who were Emergency Service (ESU) police officers at Truck 9 in Ozone Park, Queens. Emergency Service cops responded to suicide attempts off buildings or bridges, people under trains, and plane crashes, as well as any situation where it was felt their presence was needed and could not be handled by the regular precinct cops.

I wrote a letter to Deputy Commissioner Walter Arm, who was in charge of public relations for the N.Y.P.D. He set up a meeting with Assistant Chief Inspector Walter Klotzbach, head of the ESU. At that meeting, I chatted with Chief Klotzbach, who wanted to know if I knew Tom Gallagher, a dear friend and a Daily News Staff Photographer. That broke the ice, and I explained that I wanted to ride with members of Truck 9 for six months. Chief Klotzbach immediately approved and sent off the necessary paperwork.

As a result, I saw and photographed some gruesome scenes while on patrol with those elite men, and I will never forget the respect they showed me.

Riding with them was the only reason I was able to photograph an Eastern Airlines DC-7 that crashed and burned at Idlewild Airport (now JFK International) on November 30, 1962 during a dense fog, killing 27 people. The officers of Truck 9 took me right to the site of the burning aircraft. My photos of that catastrophe earned me a $100 bonus from the managing editor.

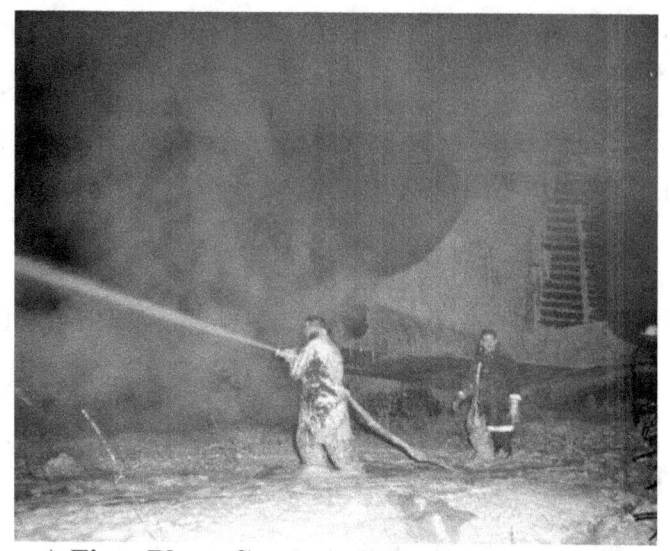

A Fiery Plane Crash At Idlewild (Now JFK).

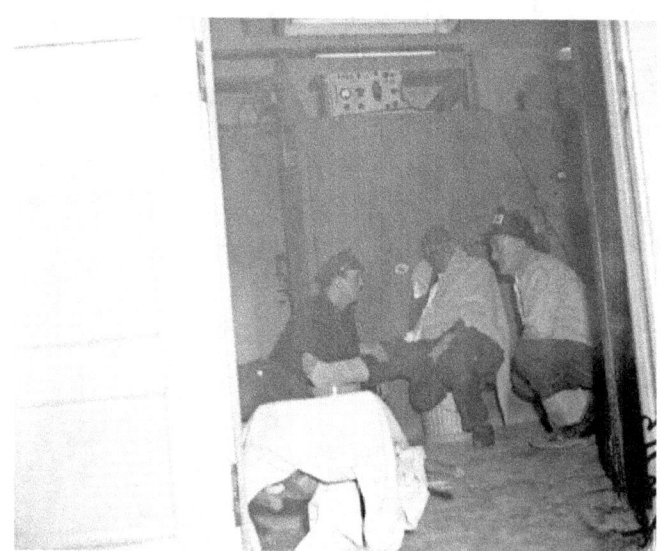

Plane Crash Survivor Being Treated.

In 1969, then Congressman Hugh Carey's two sons, Peter, 18 and Hugh Jr. 17 were killed in an auto accident on Shelter Island, some one hundred miles east of New York City, where the Carey family had a summer home. Using available light with my Rolleiflex steadied on a railing in the choir loft, I took a photo of the two caskets, side by side, in front of the church during the funeral Mass at St. Savior's Catholic Church on 8th Avenue in Brooklyn. It was a powerful photo of two brothers, whose lives were snuffed out in an instant, as they lay next to each other in God's house while their father eulogized them.

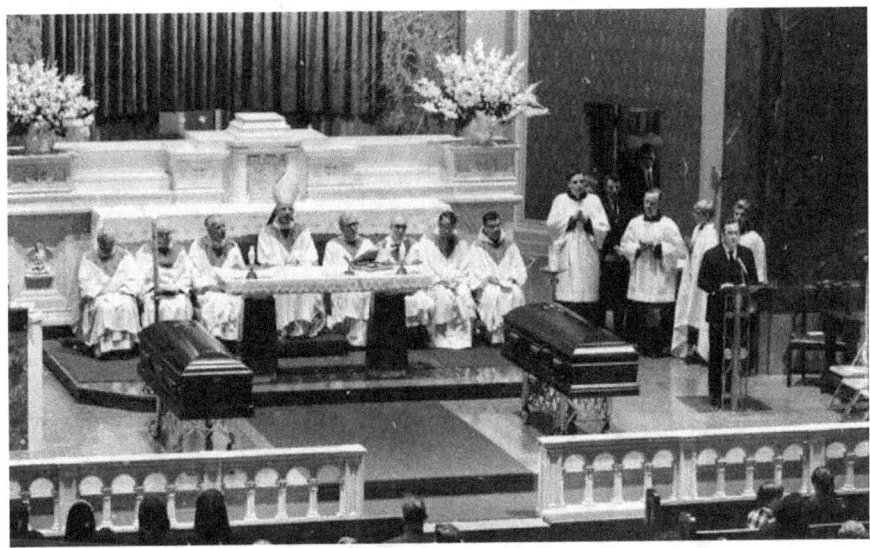

Hugh Carey Eulogizes His Two Sons.

As will be shown in subsequent photos, Hugh Carey persevered, and went on to become a two-term Governor of New York State in 1972, although I am sure he never got over his loss.

On October 17, 1966, a five-alarm fire raged out of control on 23rd Street in Manhattan, killing 12 firemen when a wall collapsed and trapped them in the cellar. It was the worst disaster in the New York City Fire Department's history before 9/11, when 343 firemen died at the World Trade Center in the wake of terrorist attacks.

I went to the building next door and got out on the fire escape on the second floor. A young police officer approached me and said the Fire Chief wanted me removed from my spot. I politely told him that the owner of the building, whom I pointed out, gave me permission to be there. And, I told the cop, that if it weren't for the Chief ordering his men into the inferno, 12 New York City Firemen would be alive. The officer thanked me and left. I got my pictures.

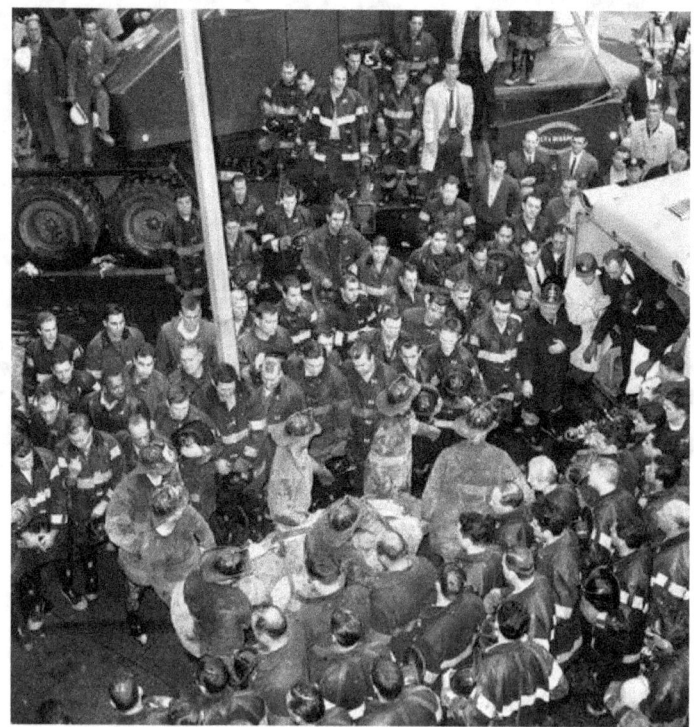

12 Firemen Died!

NO GOOD DEED …

Another assignment that stands out in my mind while working the night shift in Manhattan involved Frank Walker, a good Samaritan named Walker had a severe foot injury suffered in an auto accident that killed in his wife in 1973, leaving him with five children to look after.

On January 29, 1975, Walker went to visit his cousin in St. Vincent's Hospital. A shot rang out and a uniformed policeman staggered out and hit the wall, bleeding from a bullet wound fired from a prisoner who stole the cop's gun and shot him in the gut. Walker spotted the wounded officer and the young gunman, identified as nineteen-year-old Raymond Tubar. Walker told him to drop the gun. Instead, Tubar shot Walker. Then, as the dying man lay on the floor, Tubar fired a second bullet into him.

More police arrived and captured Tubar.

I was assigned to head out to the Walker residence in Jackson Heights, Queens, to get some photos of the Walker kids. When I arrived, the five children were with an uncle and a parish priest. The children, with their shocked and sad faces, stared out at me. As Jim Bishop wrote in the March 1976 issue of Readers Digest: "No one can predict what will move a metropolis to pity. In this case, one photo did it."

Walker was given a full Inspector's Funeral, the first in the Police Department's history for a civilian. Mayor Abe Beame, along with many dignitaries, attended the funeral, where some 2,500 police officers saluted the good Samaritan who gave his life for one of their own. Donation sites were set up at all police precincts in the city. All in all, the amount totaled $440,000, a huge amount in those days.

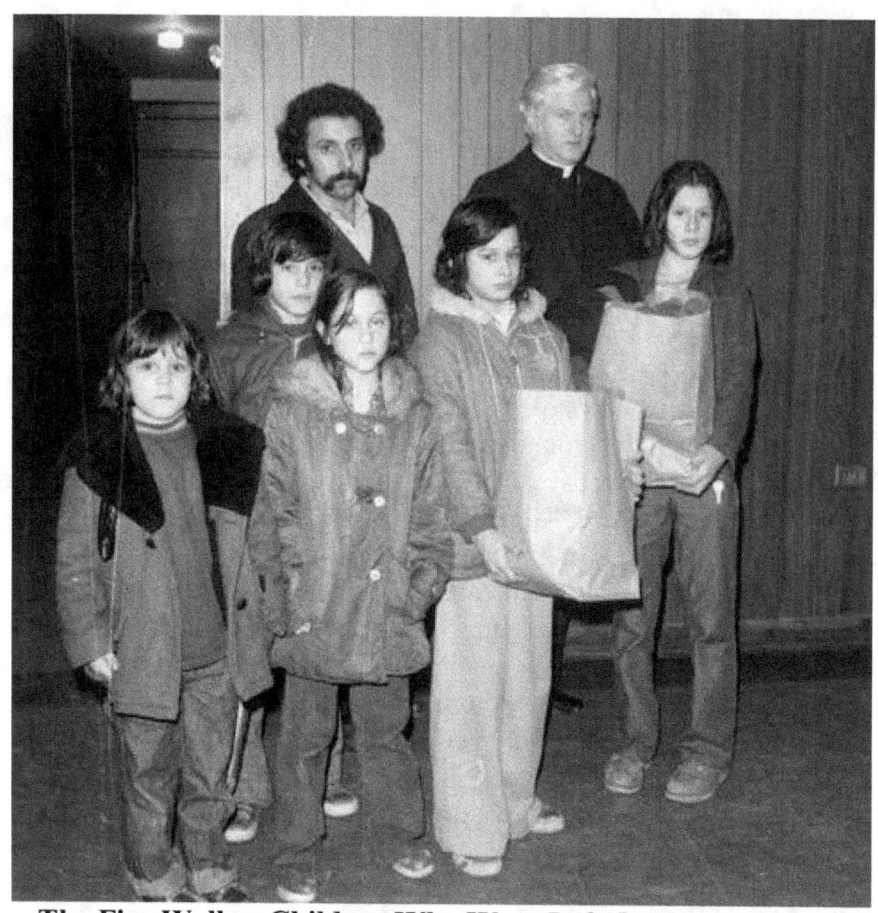

The Five Walker Children Who Were Left Orphans After Their Father Was Shot To Death Saving A Policeman's Life. Behind Them Is Their Uncle, Ralph Capone, And Father Frank Mcdonough Of St. Joan Of Arc Catholic Church In Queens.

When the shack's phone jingled one day, the lieutenant said there was a man threating to jump off the Manhattan Bridge, which connects Brooklyn and Manhattan. I raced to scene, and sure enough, a man was clinging to the elevated train tracks, 135 feet above the East River. Traffic was halted, trains were stopped, and power shut off as Emergency Service cops tried to talk the fellow out of taking his life. They succeeded and placed him in an ambulance for a trip to the psychiatric ward of a local hospital in Brooklyn.

I had my photos and headed back to the shack, wrote the captions and gave them to our messenger, Teddy DeDonna, who took them to the main office on 42nd street for processing.

About two hours later I looked out of the office window and there was the "jumper" I had just photographed speaking to a police officer on the steps the "seven eight" precinct, pointing up at me. The medics at the hospital must have asked him the color of George Washington's white horse and when he answered them correctly turned him loose.

Suddenly, this nut case walked into the shack. He wanted to beat the hell out of me for taking his picture! Chuck Frattini, who had served in the United States Marine Corps, would have none of it. He got into a slugfest with my "jumper."

I yelled to the officer on the precinct steps. He came running and together with Chuck subdued the loon and dragged him off in handcuffs to be charged with assault.

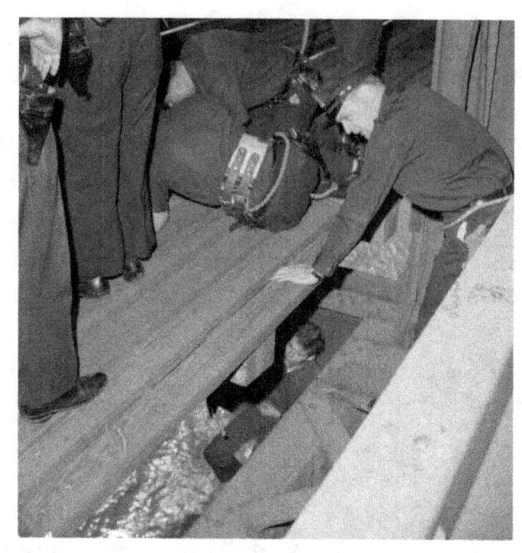

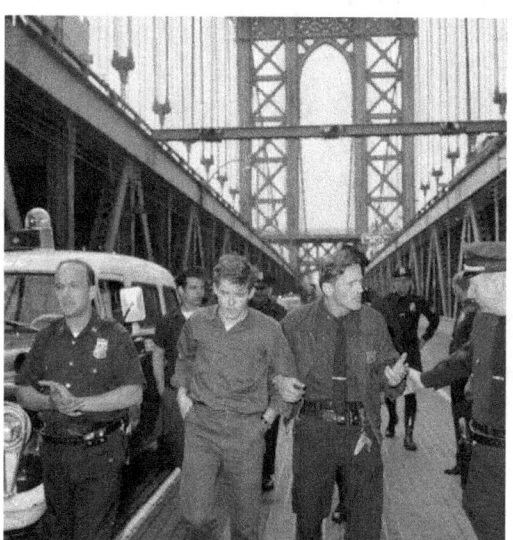

**The Cops Rescued Him From Above The East River.
Later He tried To Attack Me!**

Then there was the sad case of a man who had been shot in a holdup at his store on Utica Avenue, about a three-mile drive. Joe Kiernan predicted that "the guy will be in Walter B. Cooke's before you get there." Walter B. Cooke was a very well-known chain of funeral homes throughout New York City.

Joe did not know what a speed demon I was behind the wheel. I arrived on the scene before the ambulance and made photos of the emergency service police officers working in vain to revive the man, who had no apparent wound. They rolled him over onto his stomach and lifted his shirt. They discovered the fatal bullet wound in his back.

Back at the shack I good-naturedly told Joe that I beat Walter B. Cooke!

***

It was a quiet morning on September 28, 1976 when two masked gunmen, armed with a shotgun and pistol, announced a holdup at the Bank of North America in Ridgewood, Queens.

After scooping up $14,000, they spotted two New York City cops, officers Richard Carey and Joseph Gloss, waiting outside, and gunfire erupted between the hero cops and bandits. The thugs fled on foot to a car waiting for a traffic light and shot the driver, Donald Gormanly, 32, in the head and threw him out of the car. They escaped with the cops in hot pursuit for about eight miles with shots being exchanged between the robbers and police. In the back seat of the hijacked auto was Mrs. Susan Gormanly, 26, with her four-month-old twin daughters.

The chase ended when the bandits abandoned the car in Forest Hills and escaped on foot. Mrs. Gormanly and the twins were not injured, and her husband was treated and released from a local hospital after stitches in his head sealed the wound from the bullet that grazed his scalp.

Some 20 shots were fired between police and the fleeing suspects who were not apprehended.

AN AMAZING STORY!

The next four photos detail the aftermath of a bank robbery and subsequent kidnapping of the Gormanly twin baby girls, who were in a car with their parents when the bandits carjacked it.

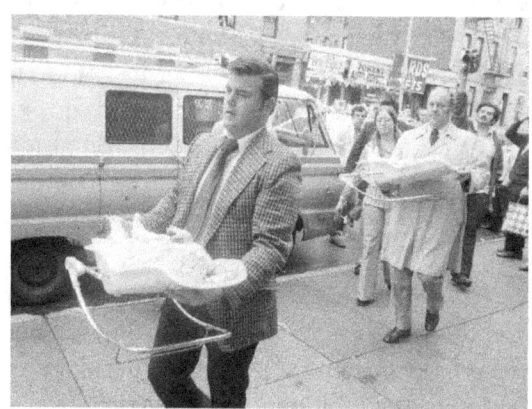

Detectives Carry Rescued Infants.

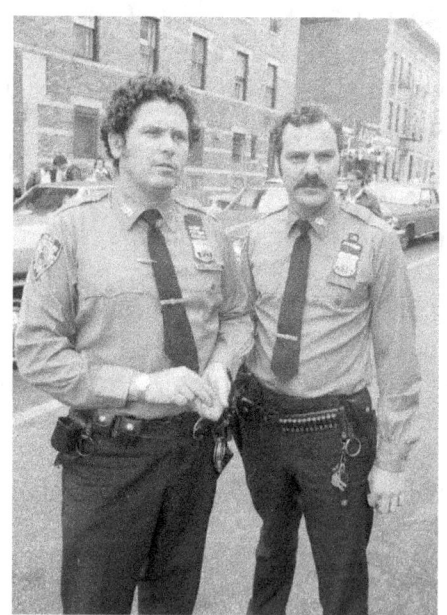

Officers Richard Carey (L) And Joseph Gloss Exchanged Fire With The Robbers.

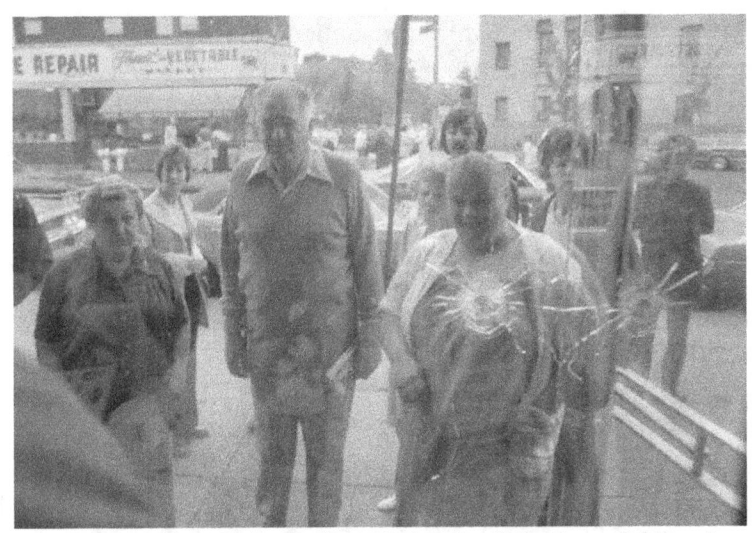

Passersby Look At Bullet Holes In Window Of Bank.

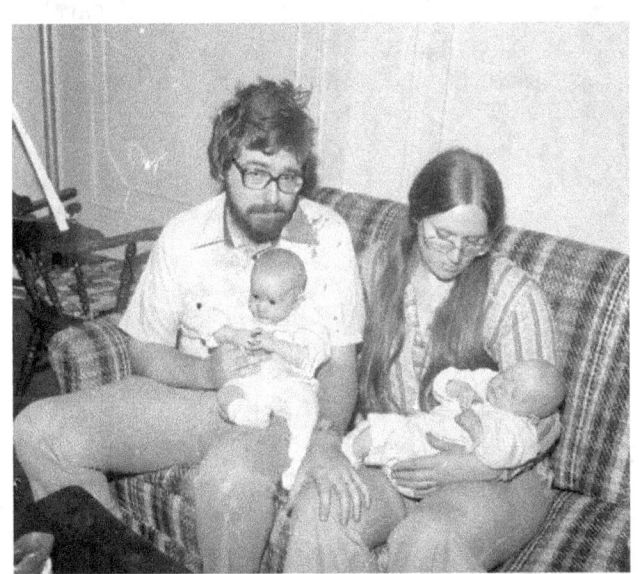

**Donald And Susan Gormanly With Their Twins.
Donald Had Been Treated For A Scalp Wound.
Blood Can Be Seen On The Left Shoulder Of His Shirt.**

One time, a call came through about a cat stuck behind a radiator in the Park Slope neighborhood. I responded to the address and chatted with the precinct cops, who were waiting for the Emergency Service (EMS) officers to unhook the radiator and free the animal, which managed to get stuck in the basement of a three-story brownstone. We all looked at the situation, and indeed the black cat (of course!) was stuck between the wall and the radiator. The EMS men got a big Stillson wrench to unhook the radiator when I noticed an inlet/outlet on the bottom of the fixture. If they opened the connection, three stories of water from above would flush out of that disconnected joint.

The EMS men said, "It's summer, so the system is empty." I disagreed, as my dad had told me about the difference between hot water and steam heating systems. The hot water system was always full, summer or winter. This did not deter the cops, and when they broke the connection, that 1,200 lb., five-foot, cast-iron radiator spun around like a toy, flooded the basement. The cat flew out the door, never to be seen again.

I never said a word to the officers. My smile said it all.

MEMORABLE ASSIGNMENT

One very memorable assignment I covered while in Brooklyn was of a fireman named Dan Tracy, who had saved a child from a burning building the night before. I was given his name and the address of the firehouse, and told to go find him.

It was a beautiful summer day on July 27, 1967 as I parked at Ladder 120 on Watkins Street and asked if Dan Tracy was still working. He was, and his lieutenant gave me permission to take the hero fireman with me to find the infant. I requested he only take his helmet, as it is the distinguishing mark of a fireman.

We found the child, Terry Sykes, 7 months old, at a relative's house. I asked Tracy to put on his helmet and raise him up as high as he could. He obliged, and the infant loved it, smiling from ear to ear.

It made the cover of the paper, and the Uniformed Firemen's Association used it on billboards and newspaper ads to educate people in certain neighborhoods that firemen were their friends. In those days, chain link fences were jury rigged around fire trucks to protect them from projectiles that were thrown from rooftops as firemen men rushed to the scene of an emergency.

Tracy, who rose to the rank of Captain with FDNY, passed away of cancer in January of 2014. He was known as the Fireman's Fireman and an icon to the members of Ladder120 in the Brownsville, section of Brooklyn. According to the Watkins Street FDNY website, Tracy represented the very best of the FDNY. He saw the establishment of the four-year "Fireman Daniel J. Tracy Scholarship" at St. John's University in 1976, which continues to this day. He was a three-time FDNY Medal Day Winner as well as a three-time New York Daily News "Hero of the Month Award" winner for his bravery.

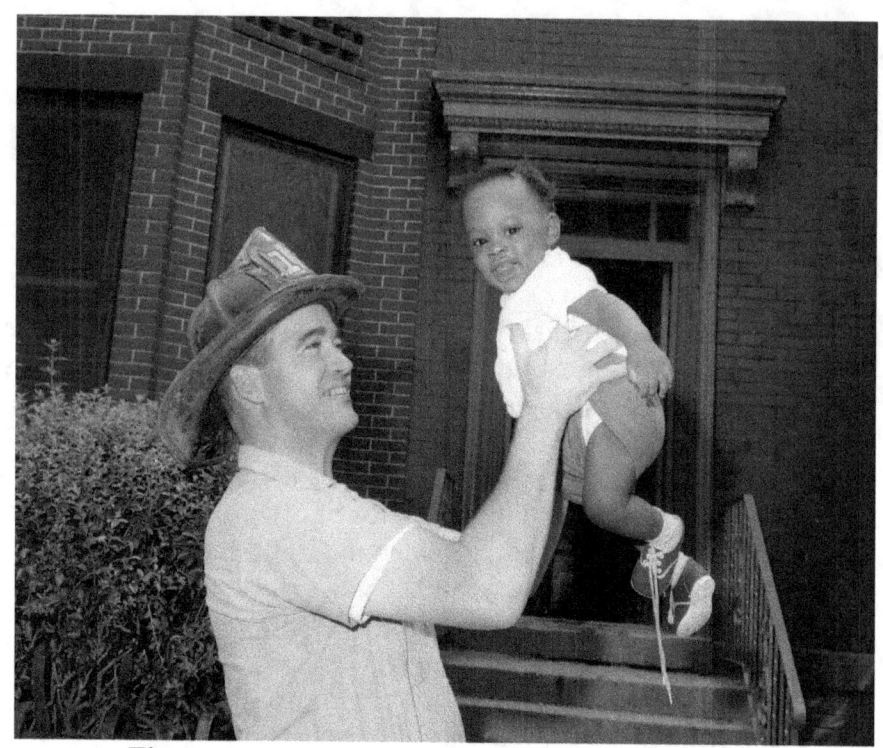
Fireman Dan Tracy With Baby Terry Sykes.

Another great assignment involved the theft of "Tarzan & Jane," two chimpanzees from the Prospect Park Zoo in Brooklyn. Press coverage was all over the story for days when someone phoned police and said that the chimps could be found in a phone booth on a Brooklyn street corner. Sure enough, cops spotted the missing pair and reunited them with their zookeeper. I took photos of the two as they "read about their kidnapping" in the Daily News.

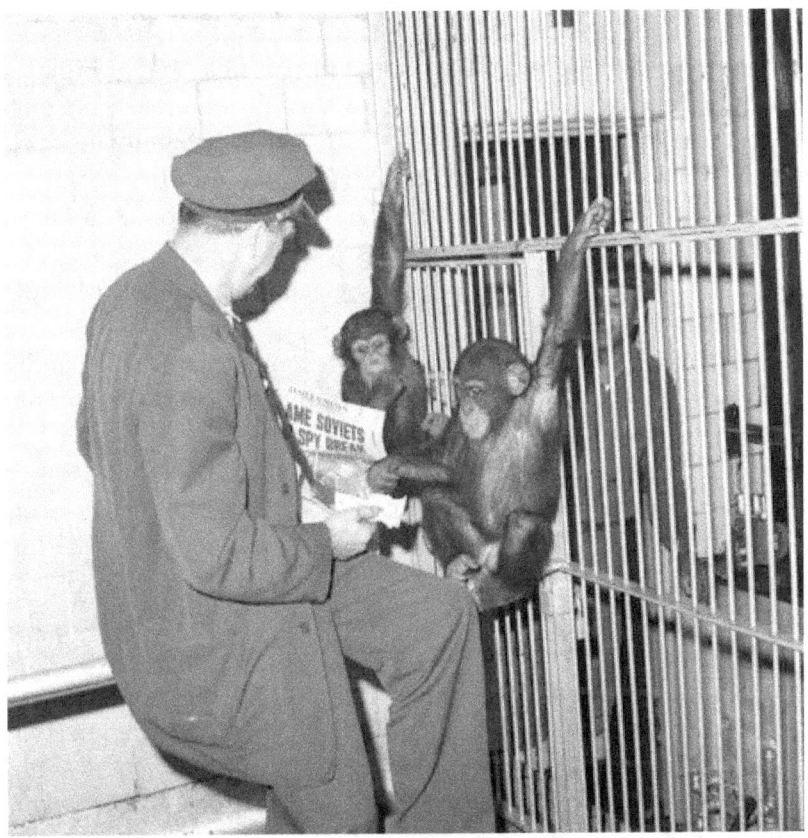

Kidnapped Chimps Aping For The Camera.

I worked in Brooklyn for approximately two years and then was transferred back to the main office in Manhattan, working the 5 pm to 1 am shift. It was a good shift, being assigned to cover many of the Mets games, the New York Rangers and Islanders hockey games, as well as boxing and Knicks basketball at Madison Square Garden.

It wasn't always a piece of cake!

While covering the Islanders at the Nassau Veterans Coliseum from the penalty box, I was hit in the head with a puck and woke up in the ambulance. Hospital X-rays showed that I had a concussion. Then, two weeks later, while covering the Monday Night Fights at Madison Square Garden in Manhattan, a full-scale riot broke out after an unpopular decision. I was struck with a thrown whiskey bottle (empty of course). The New York City police arrived in droves. They did not mess around. They went up and down the aisles, swinging their night sticks at anyone who dared to fight them. At least fifty cops took part in the melee and had it under control in less than five minutes.

Meantime, I went to the resident physician at the Garden and sat silently as he picked broken glass out of my head. Yes, the bottle broke when it hit my hard Irish head.

Another Madison Square Garden incident happened at a Ranger game. The Barnum & Bailey Circus was in town (it was performing at the Garden, but not when a Ranger game was scheduled). You can well imagine the animals doing what they had to do, and the smell in the arena was overwhelming. Some Ranger fans took it upon themselves to visit the menagerie where the animals were housed and took three 50 lb. sawdust bags to the top tier and emptied them on the opposing team as they exited when a period ended.

Needless to say, mayhem broke out as the visiting players went up into the stands with their hockey sticks. Again, the NYPD had to restore order.

You know the old joke: "I went to a fight and a hockey game broke out."

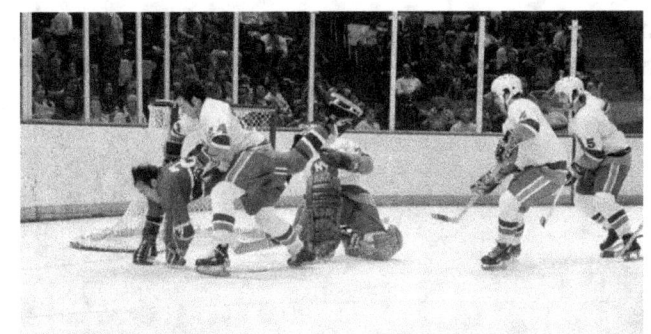

The Islanders Mix It Up At Nassau Veterans Coliseum…

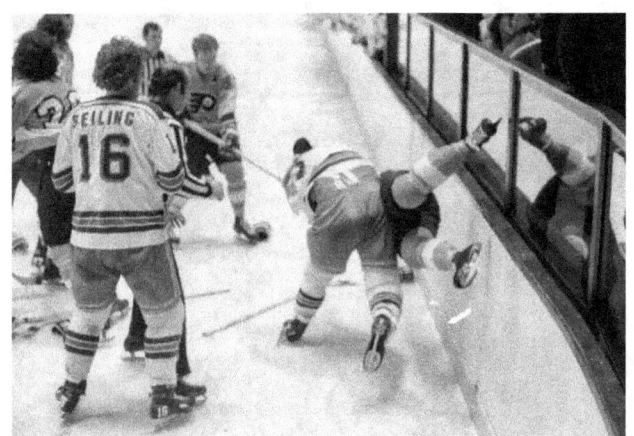

… Not To Be Outdone, The Rangers In Madison Square Garden.

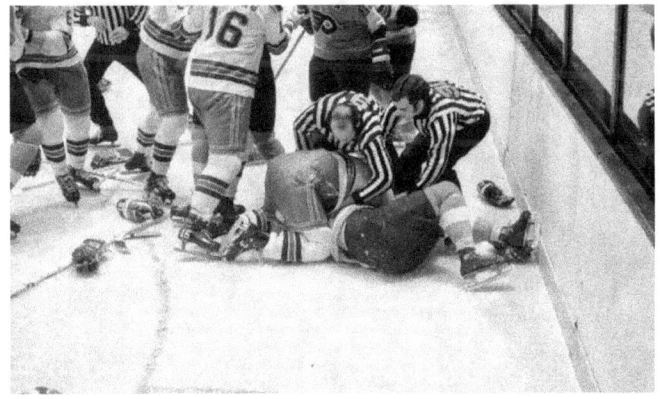

Boys Will Be Boys!

During my many years at the Daily News, I took thousands of photos of daily life in the Big Apple. Photos of celebrities, politicians, tragedies and daily life.

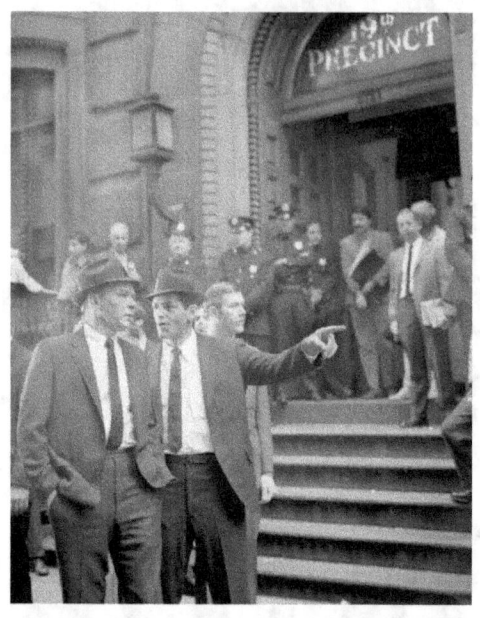

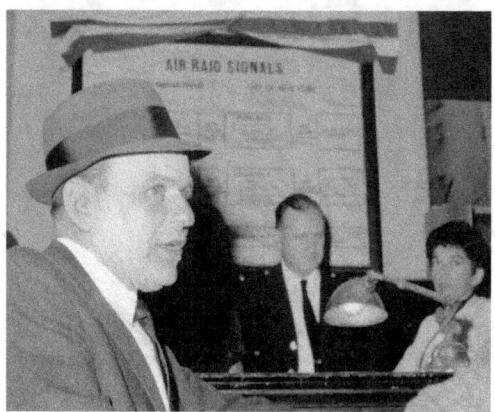

Frank Sinatra Filming 'The Detective' At The 19th Precinct.

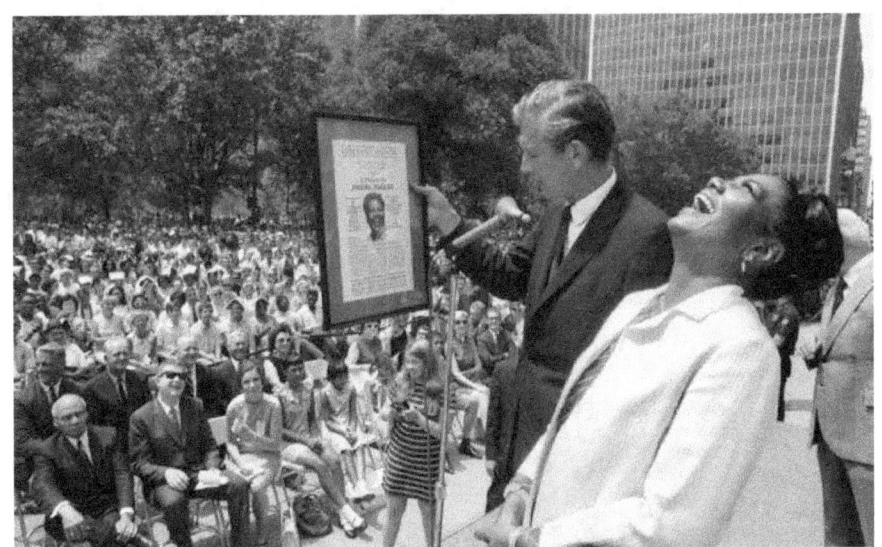

Mayor John Lindsay Honors Pearl Bailey.

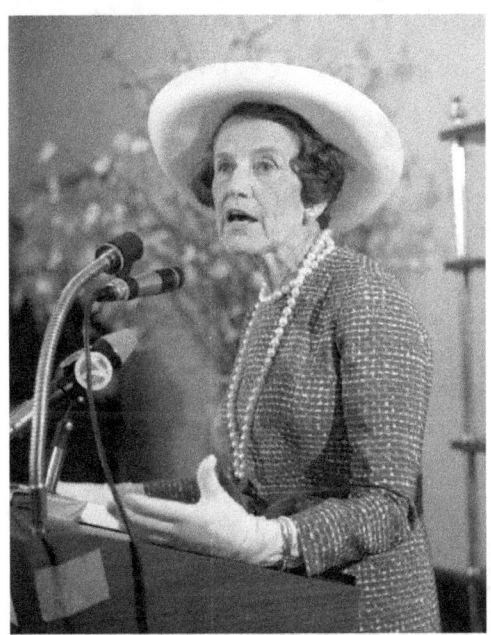

Mrs. Rose Kennedy, JFK'S Mother.

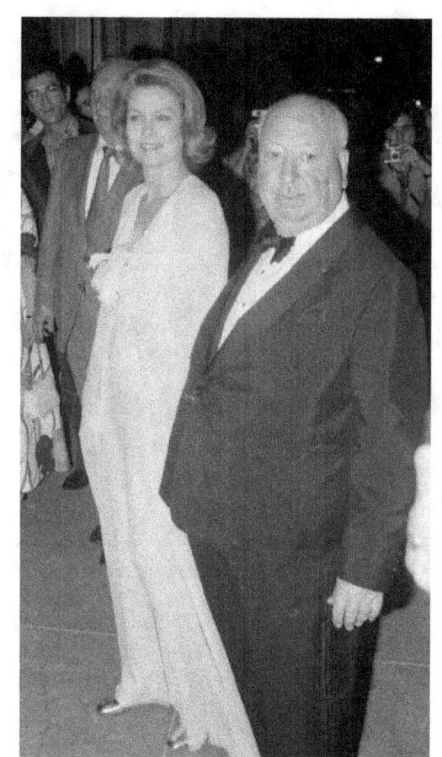

Grace Kelly And Alfred Hitchcock.

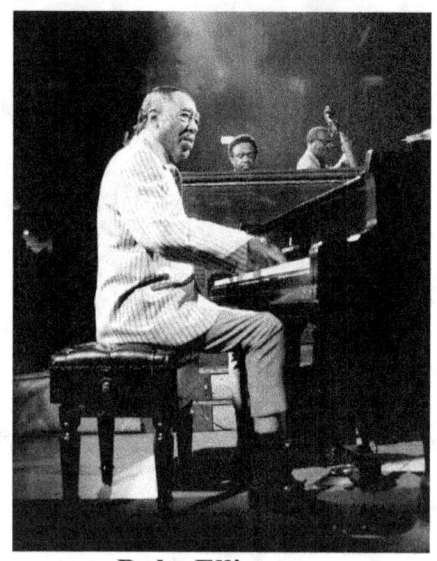

Duke Ellington.

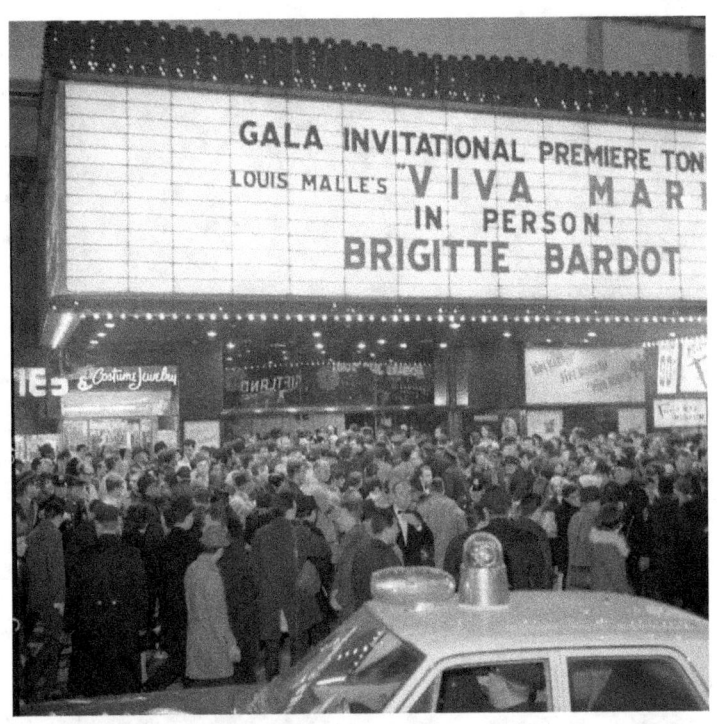

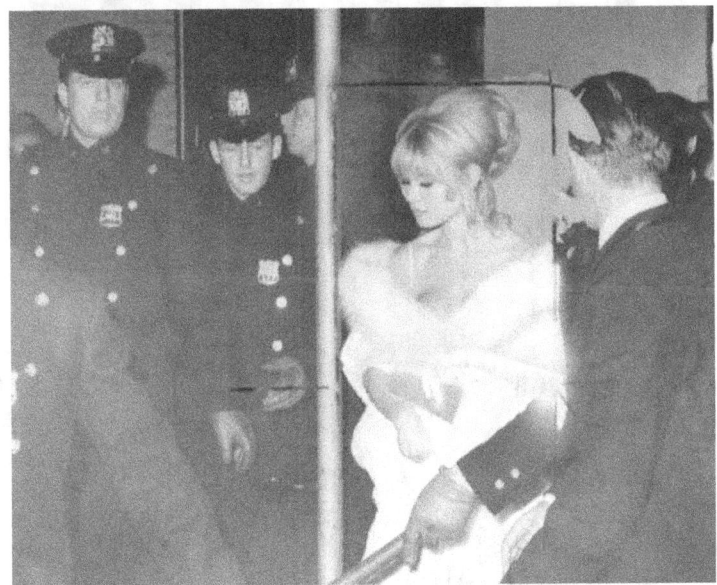

And Here She Is!

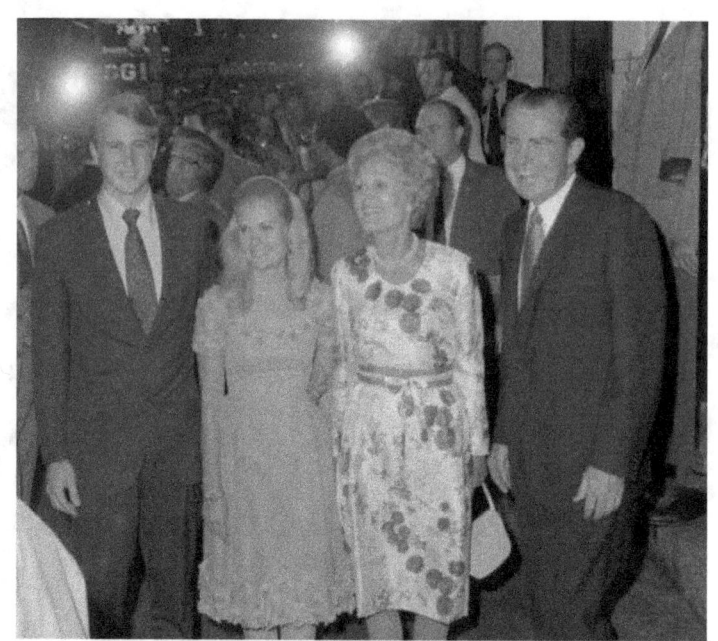
The Nixons On Broadway.

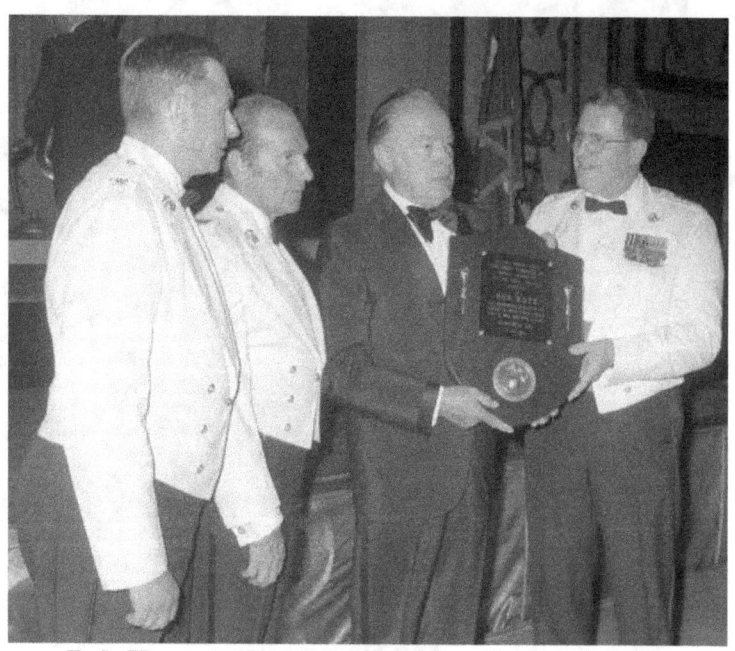
Bob Hope At The Marines' Leatherneck Ball.

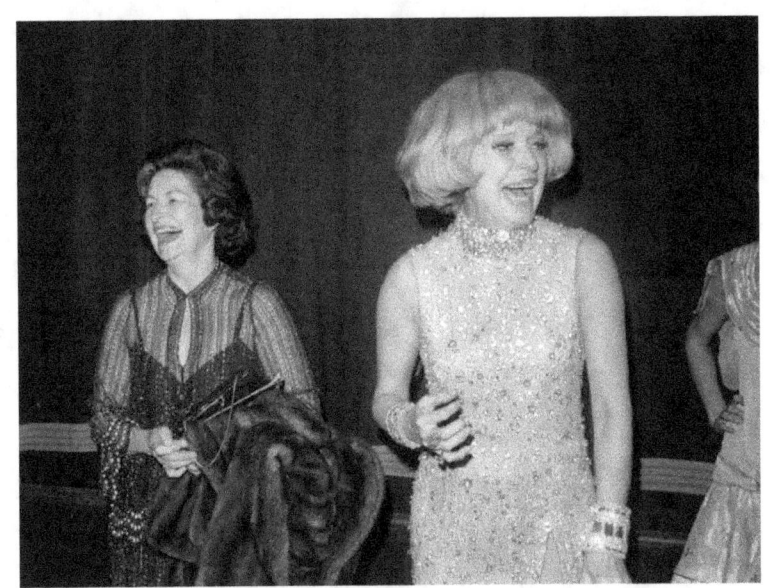

Betty Ford And Carol Channing.

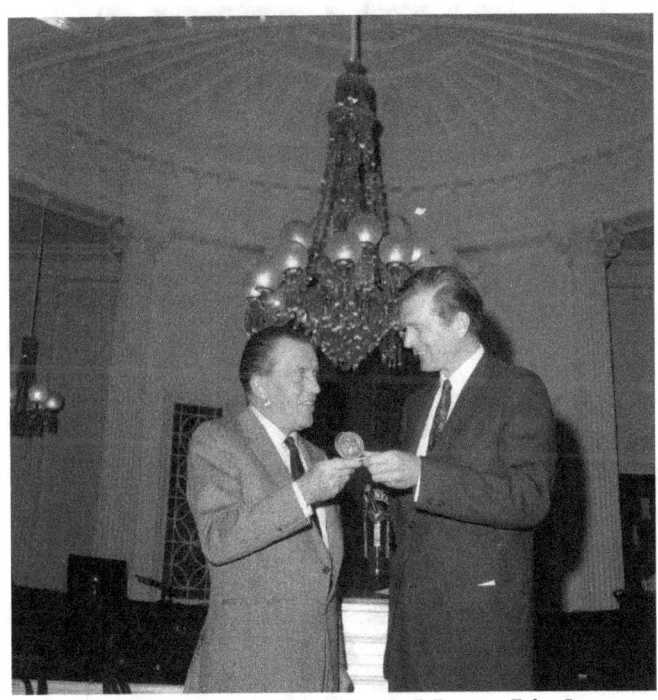

Ed Sullivan And New York Mayor Lindsay.

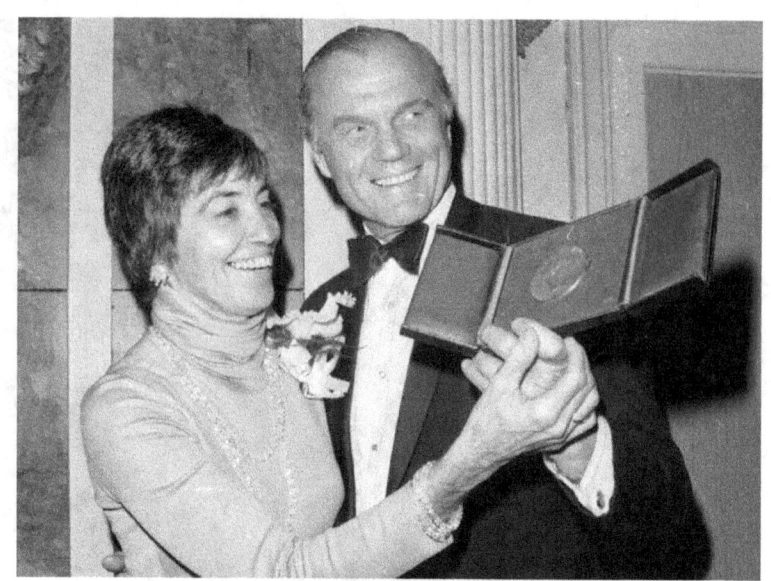

John Glenn And His Wife, Annie.

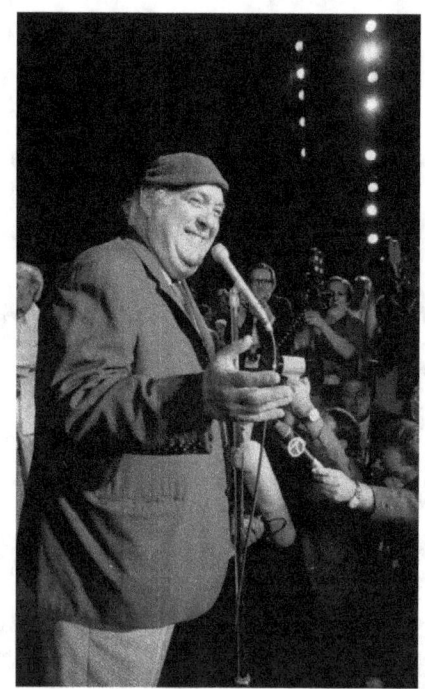

Zero Mostel.

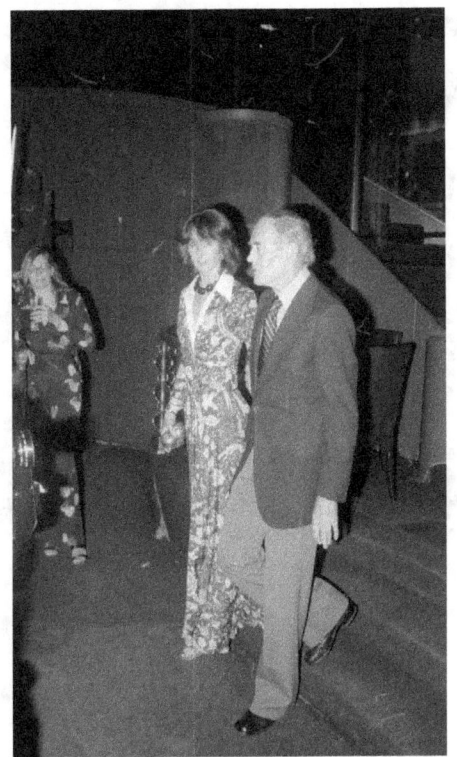
Henry Fonda And Wife.

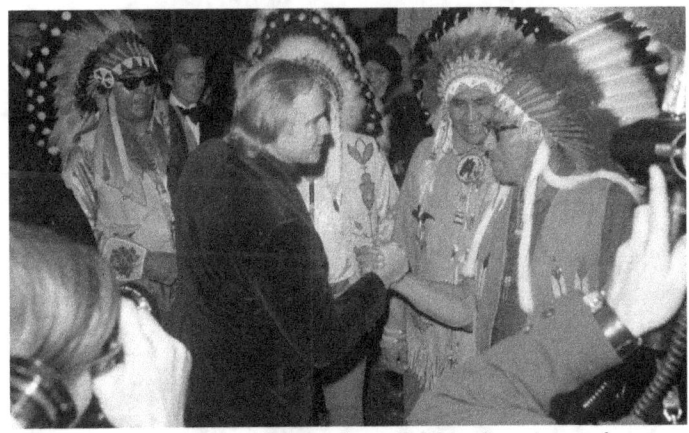
Marlon Brando, Champion Of Native Americans.

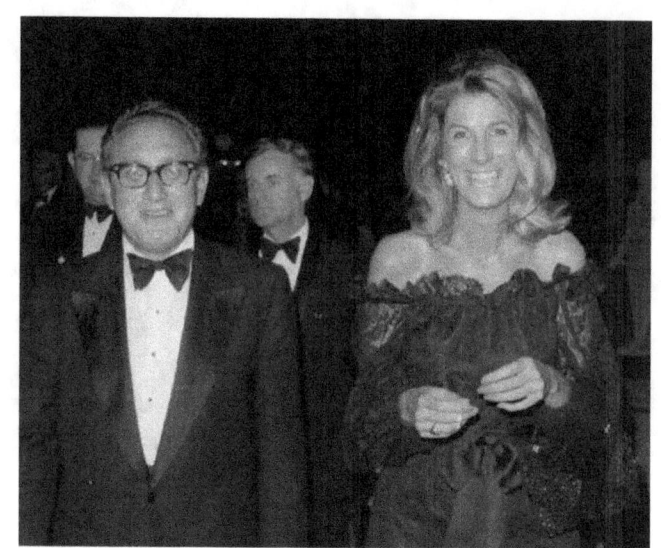

Henry And Nancy Kissinger.

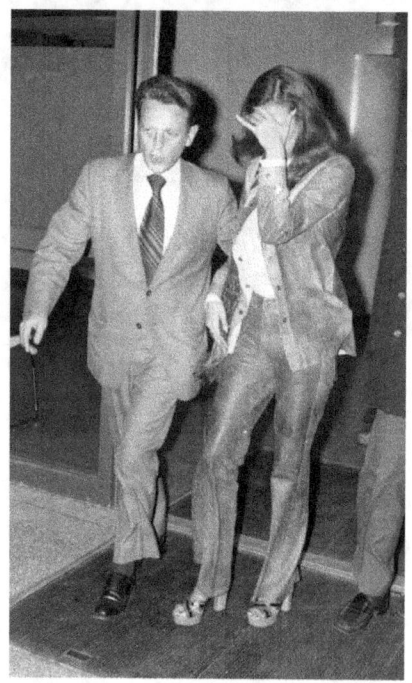

A Camera-Shy Raquel Welch.

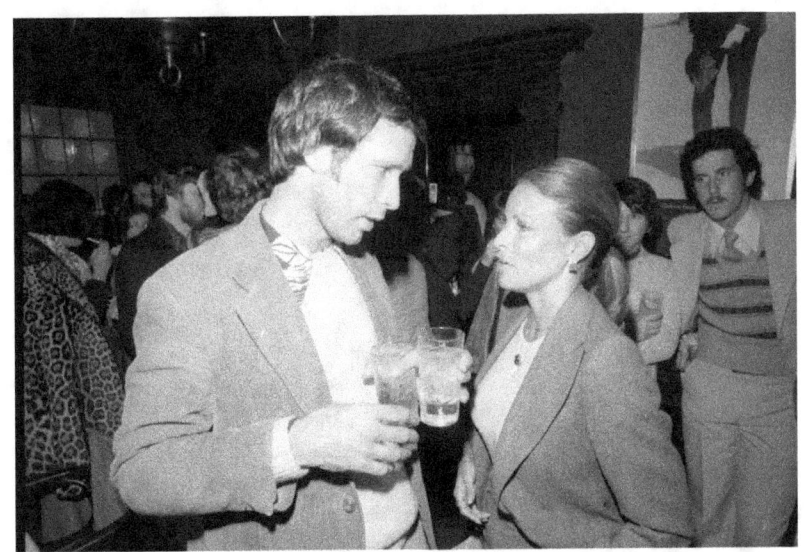
Chevy Chase.

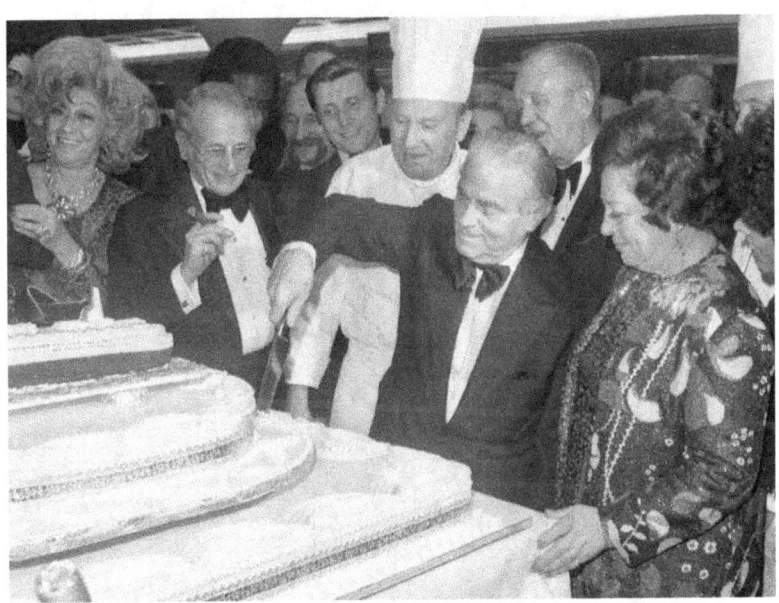
Mayor Abe Beame Cuts Cake For The QE2's Maiden Voyage.

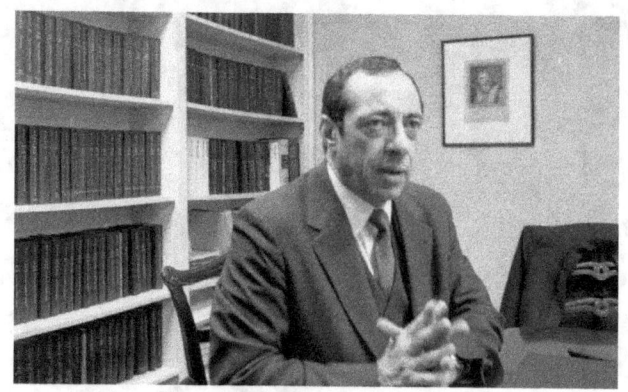

Governor Mario Cuomo.

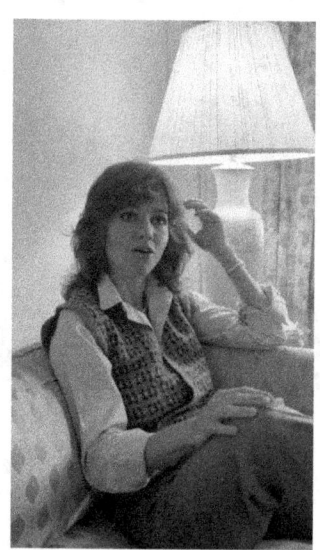

Sally Field

SAD ASSIGNMENTS FOR ALL CONCERNED

Unfortunately, covering funerals for the city's heroes is part of the job. Two of the most emotional concerned police officers, killed in the same year.

Officer Robert E. Walsh was gunned down as he tried to stop a hold up in a Queens bar in January 1981. In December, Officer Anthony Abruzzo Jr. was killed in the attempted robbery of his father-in-law as his wife looked on in horror.

Thousands of fellow officers attended the services for both hero cops.

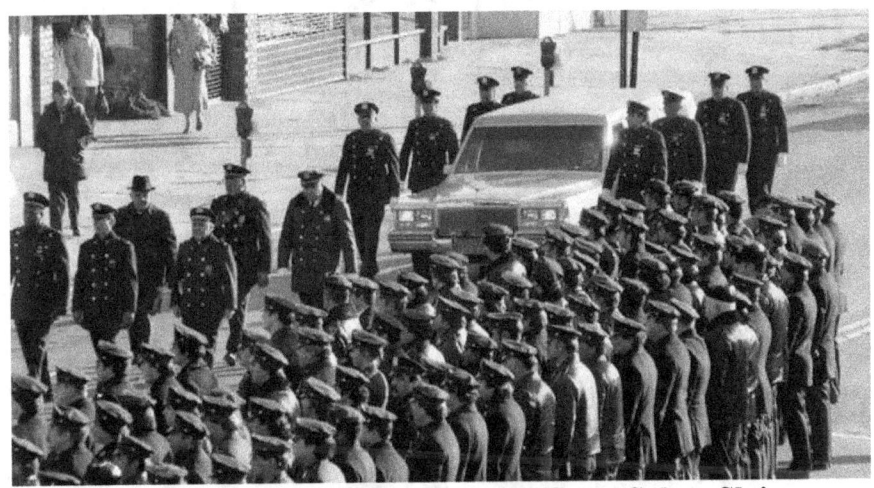

Some 2,000 New York City Police Officers Salute Slain Officer Robert E. Walsh.

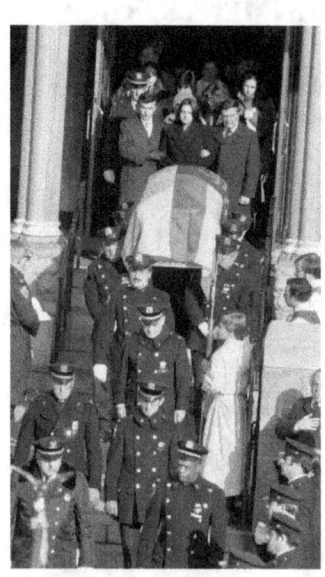

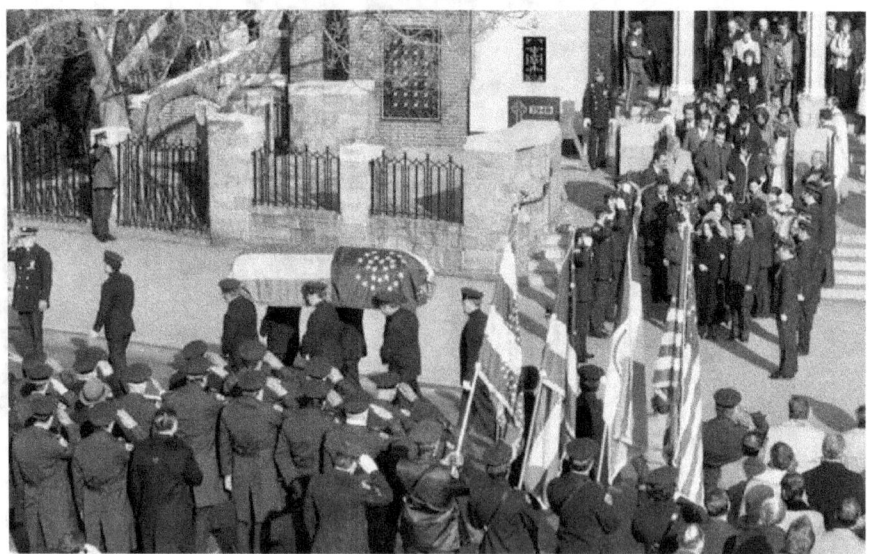

And They were There Again When Officer Abruzzo Was laid To Rest.

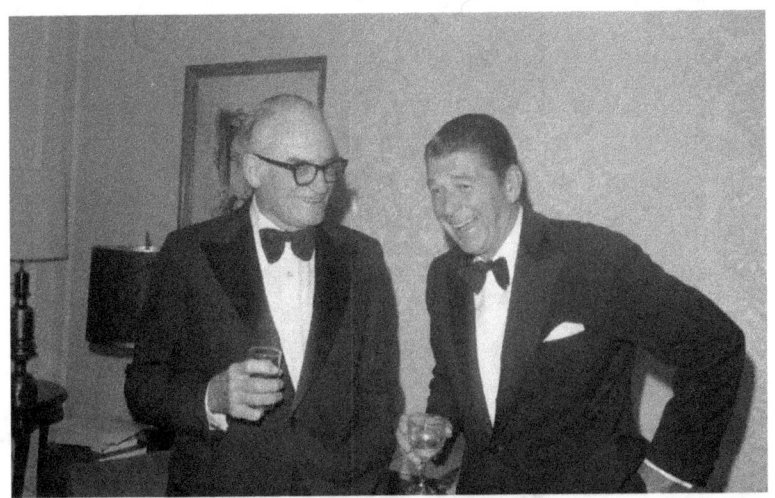

Senator Barry Goldwater And President Ronald Reagan.

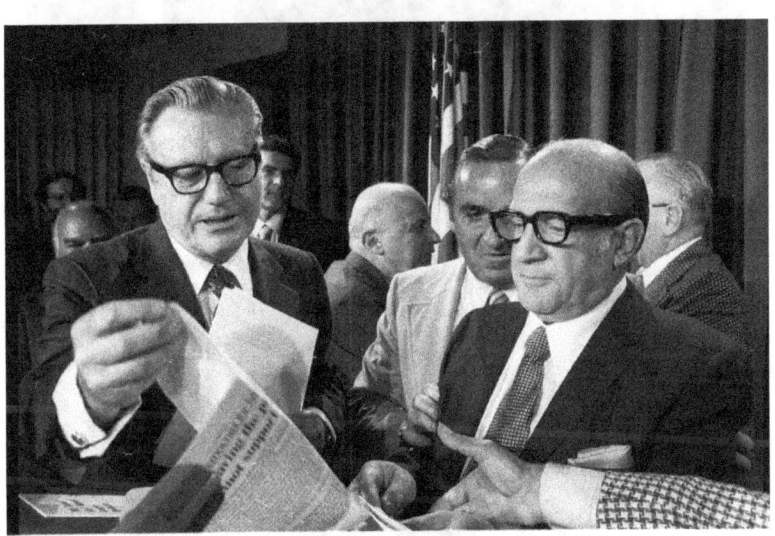

Nelson Rockefeller.

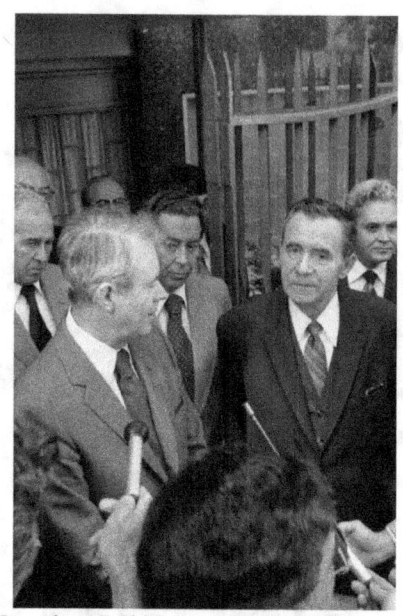

Soviet Foreign Minister Andrei Gromyko (R.)

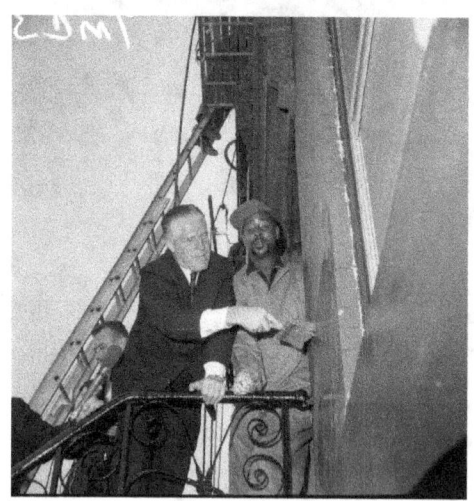

Presidential Candidate George Romney.

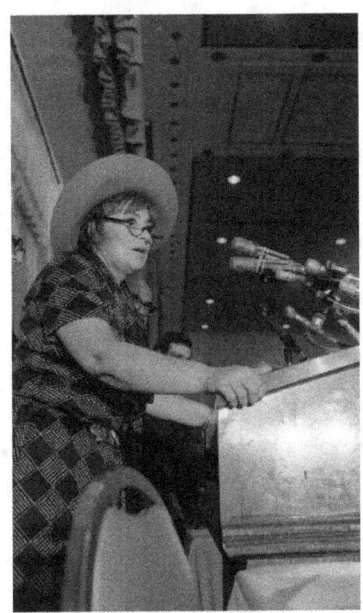

Bella Abzug.

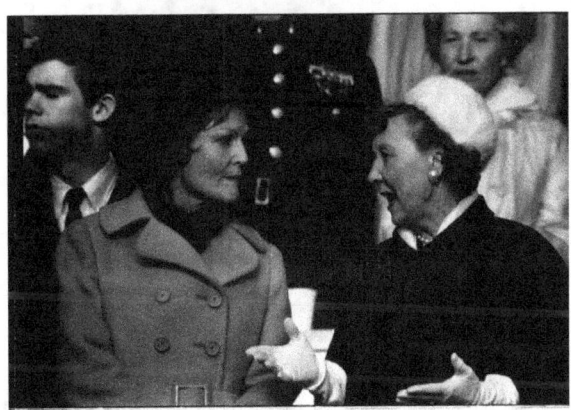

Pat Nixon And Mamie Eisenhower

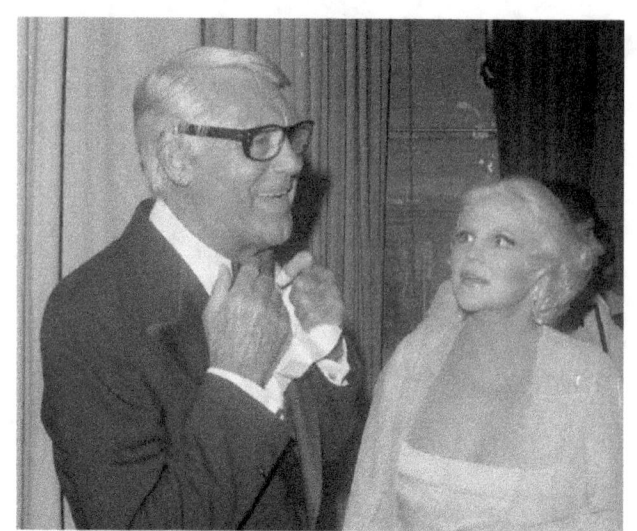

Cary Grant.

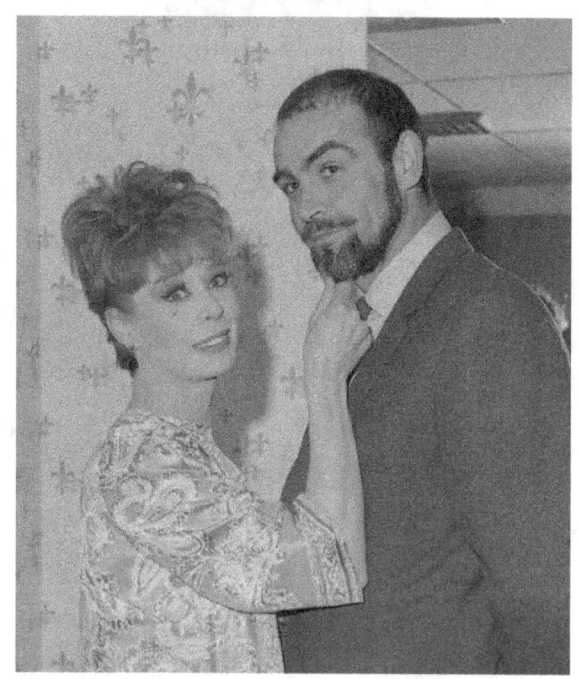

Sean Connery And Gwen Verdon

On August 7, 1974, French daredevil Phillipe Petit walked between the Twin Towers of the World Trade Center, some 1,312 feet above ground, for 45 minutes. He was then arrested by incredulous police on numerous charges. But the charges were dropped in exchange for his promise to perform a high wire act for children in Central Park.

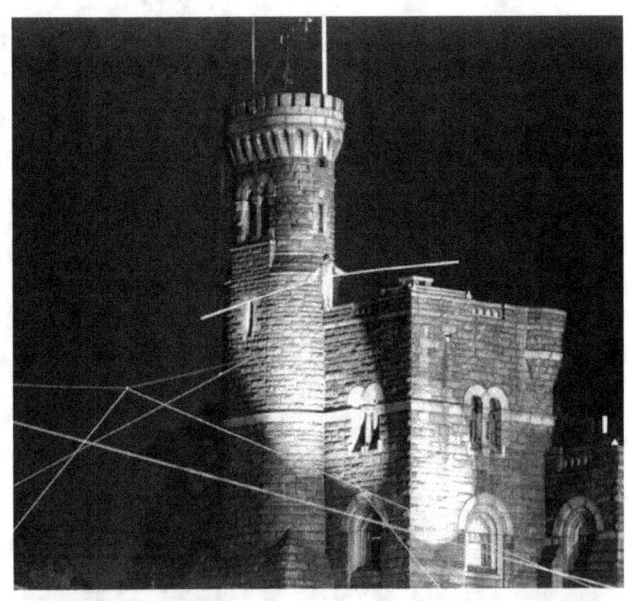

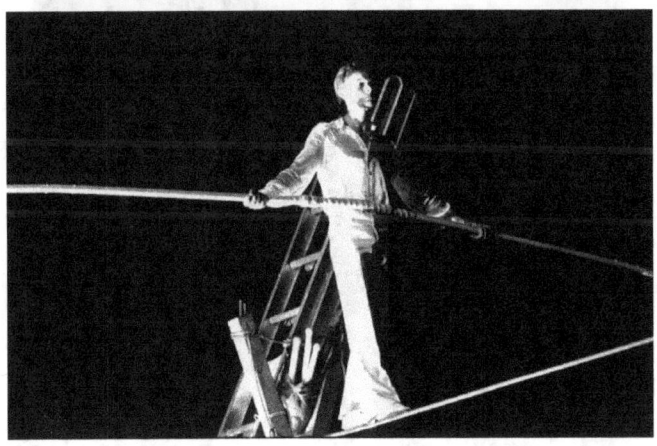

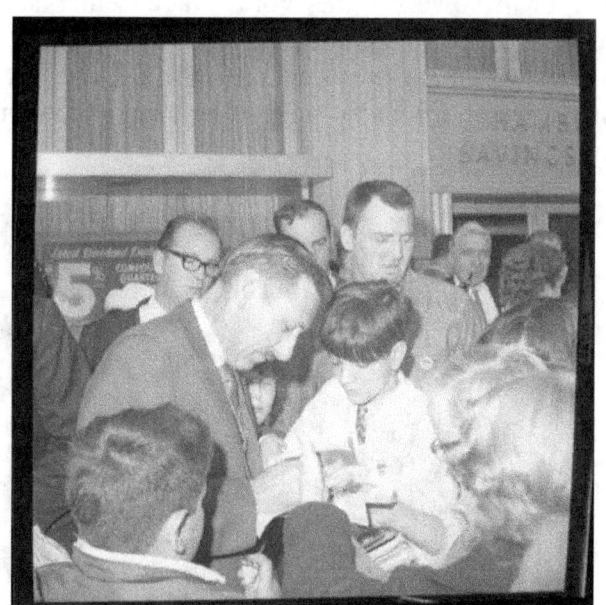

New York Yankee Manager Billy Martin.

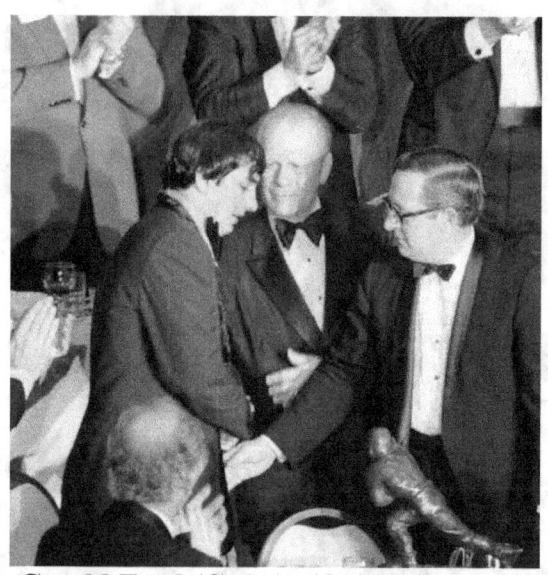

V.P. Gerald Ford (Ctr) At 1973 Heisman Dinner
For Penn State's John Cappelletti.

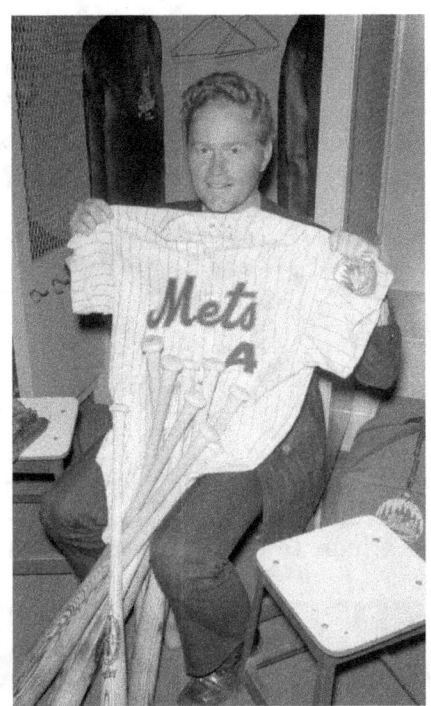
Rusty Staub Joins The Mets In 1972.

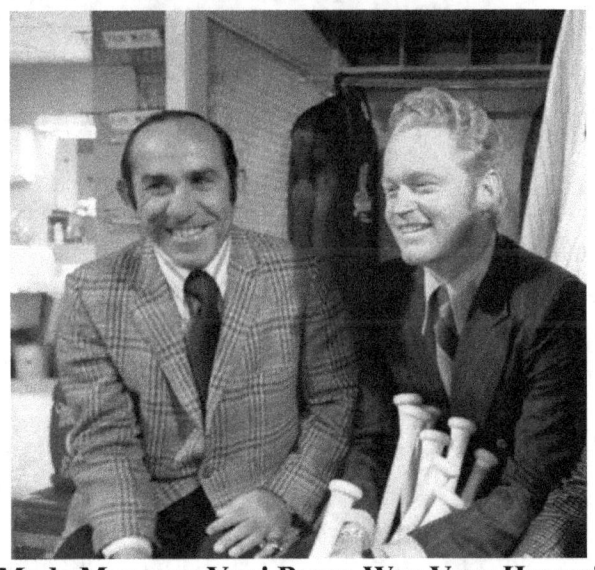
Made Manager Yogi Berra Was Very Happy!

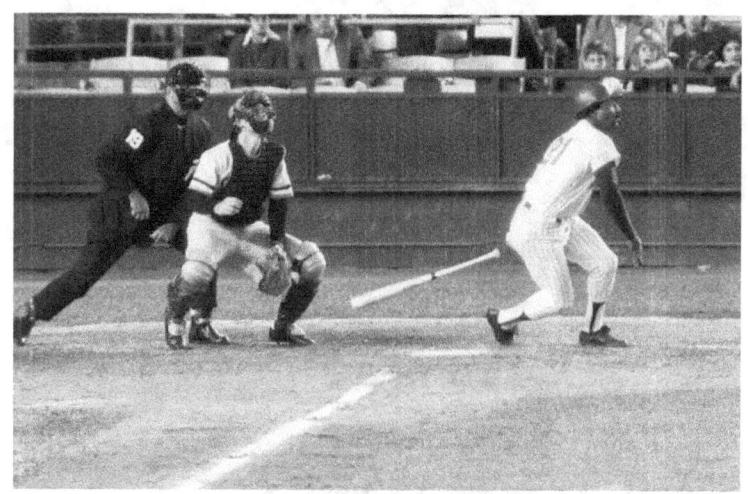

The Mets Cleon Jones Homering At Shea Stadium.

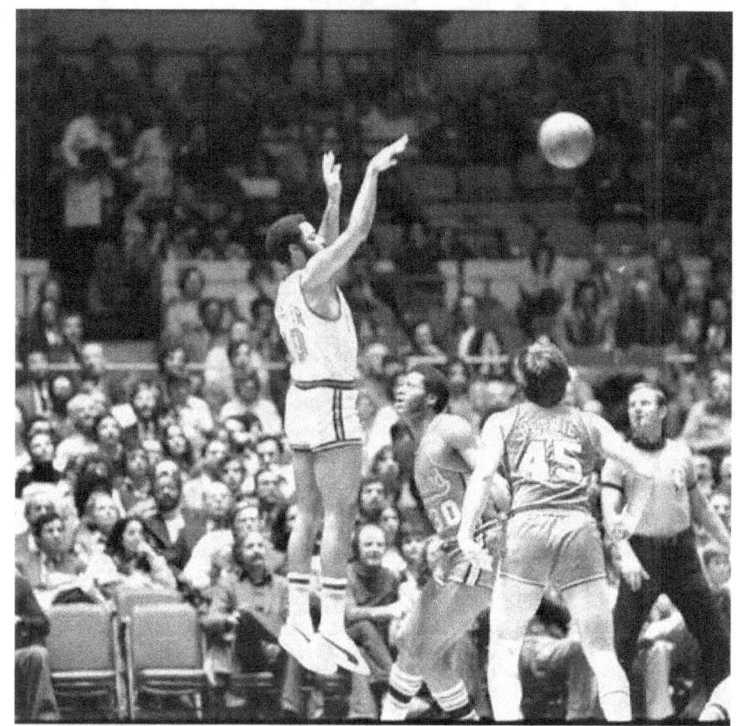

Walt (Clyde) Frazier, New York Knicks Smooth-Shooting Guard.

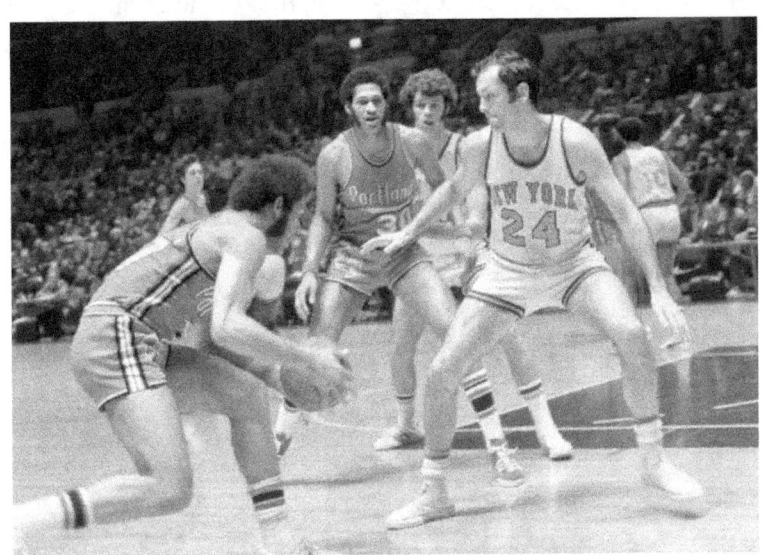

Another Famous Knick: Bill Bradley (24), Later A U.S. Senator.

There was sadness in the sports world, too. On July 6, 1975, Ruffian, perhaps the greatest thoroughbred filly ever, broke down during a "Match Race" against Foolish Pleasure at Belmont before 50,000 fans. She had to be destroyed and was buried near the finish line the next day.

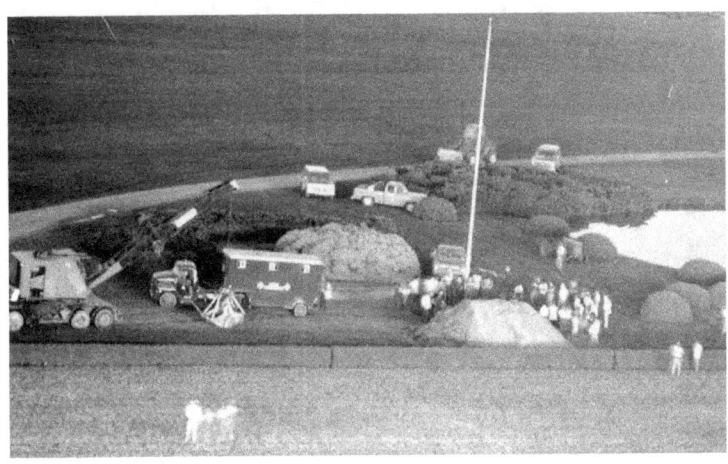

The Cardinals fleet Arnold McBride, nicknamed "Shake 'n Bake", attempts to steal second. Infielder Felix Milan gave McBride a taste of some Mets home cooking, as these shots show!

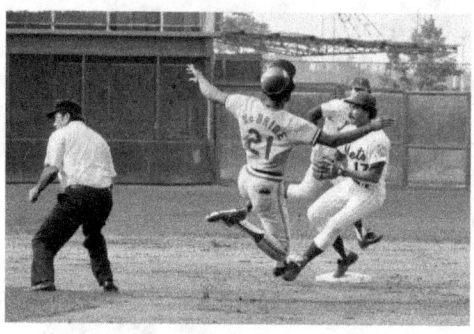

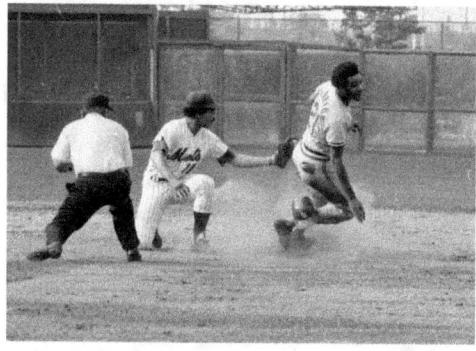

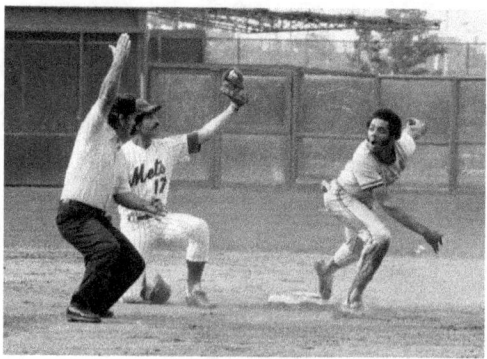

Not So Fast!

Demonstrations, against the Vietnam War and other things, were always on the menu in the volatile Big Apple.

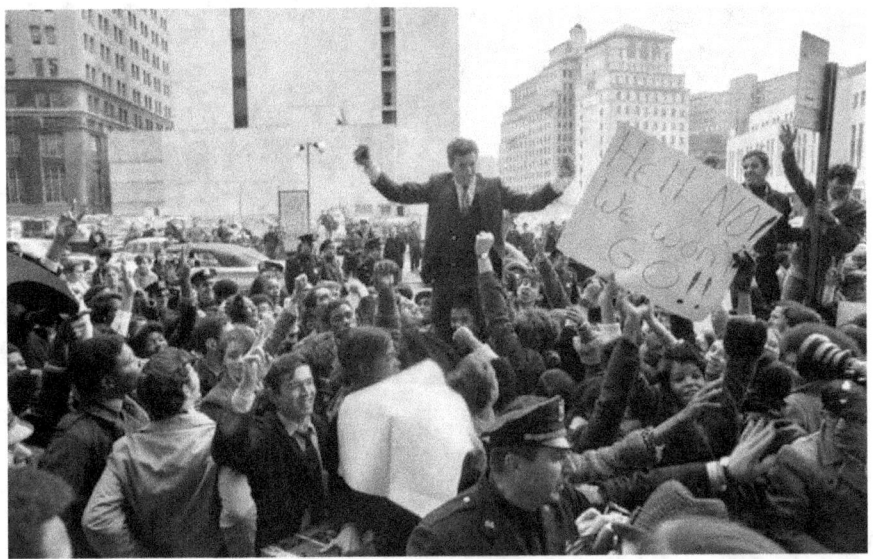

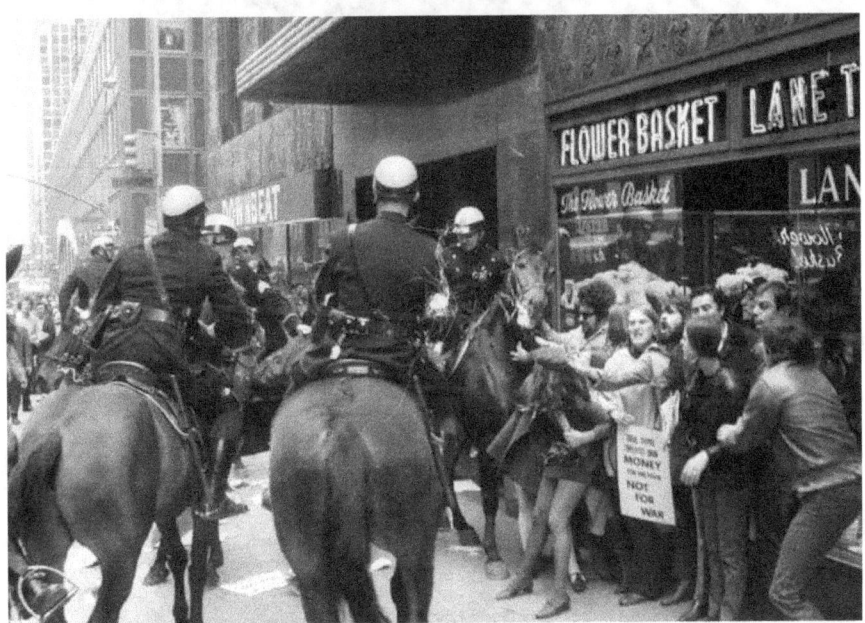

Cops Open Up Streets Blocked By Demonstrators.

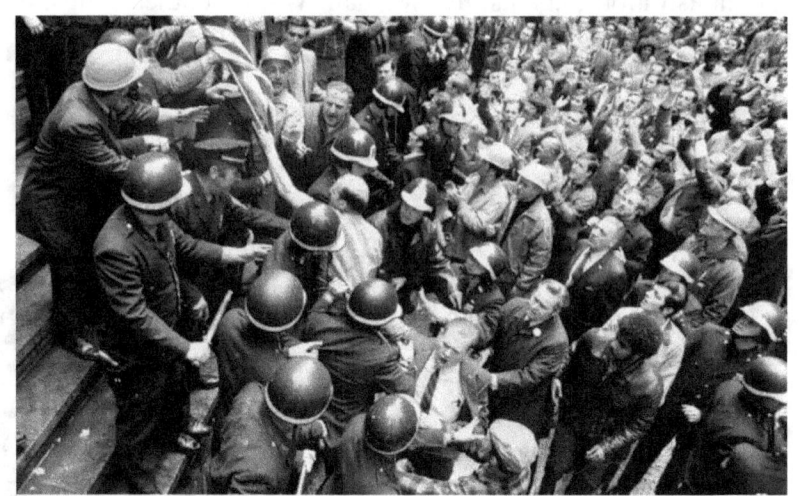

Protestors Battle Construction Workers.

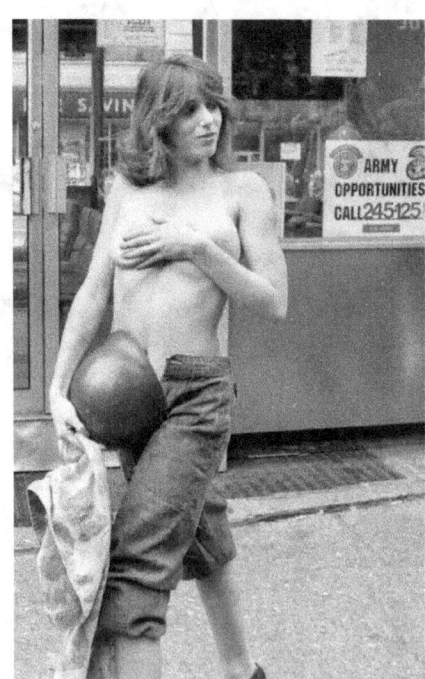

No Comment!

In 1976, Great Britain and France flew their supersonic Concorde SSTs to JFK on the same day. Local residents protesting sonic booms delayed commercial flights until the following year

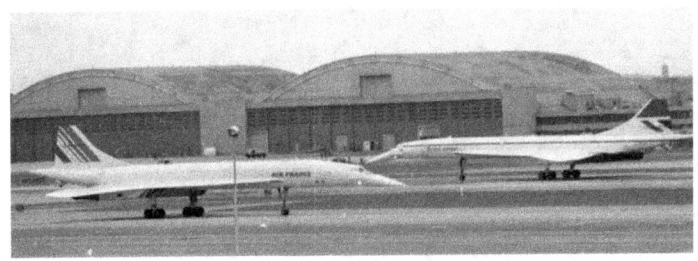

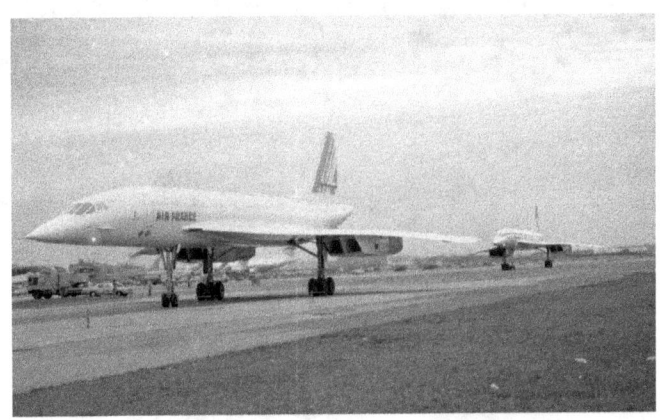

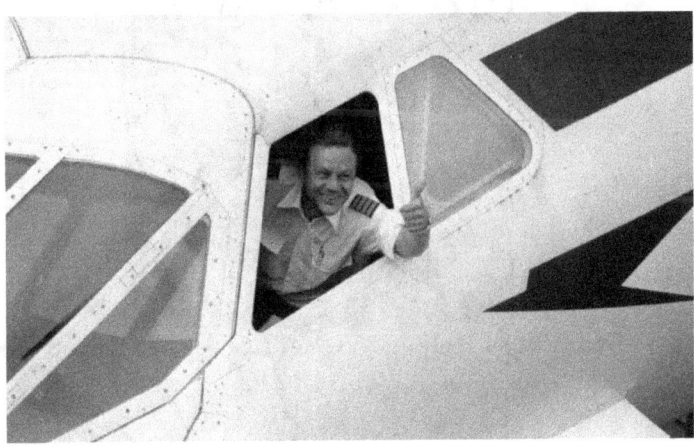

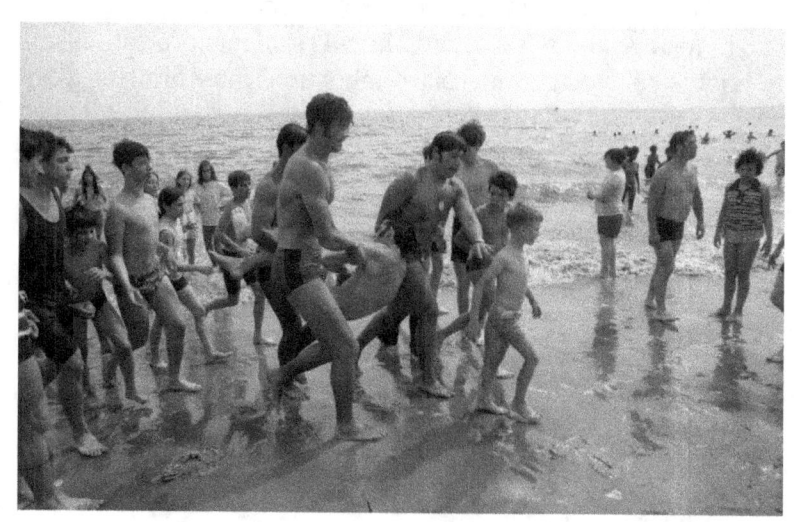

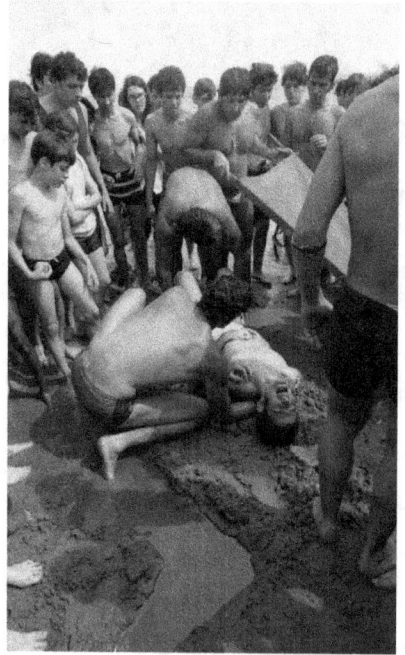

Alert Swimmers Helped With A Successful Beach Rescue.

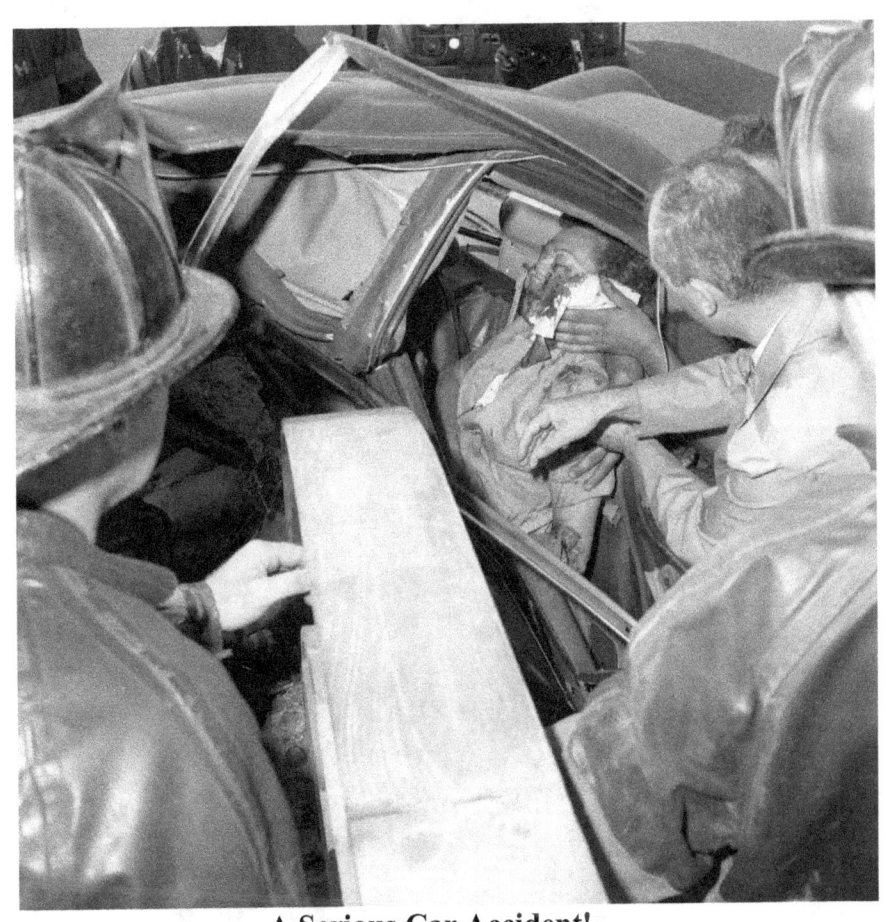

A Serious Car Accident!

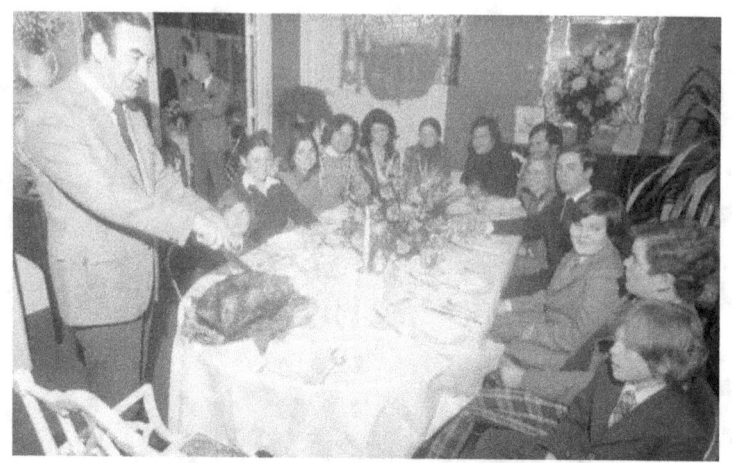

Governor Hugh Carey In Happier Times

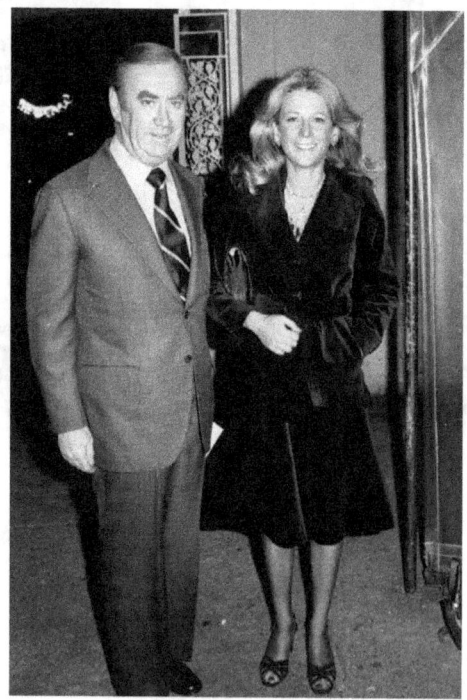

With Anne Ford

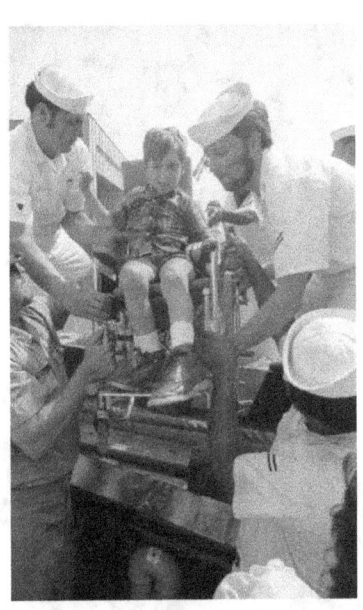

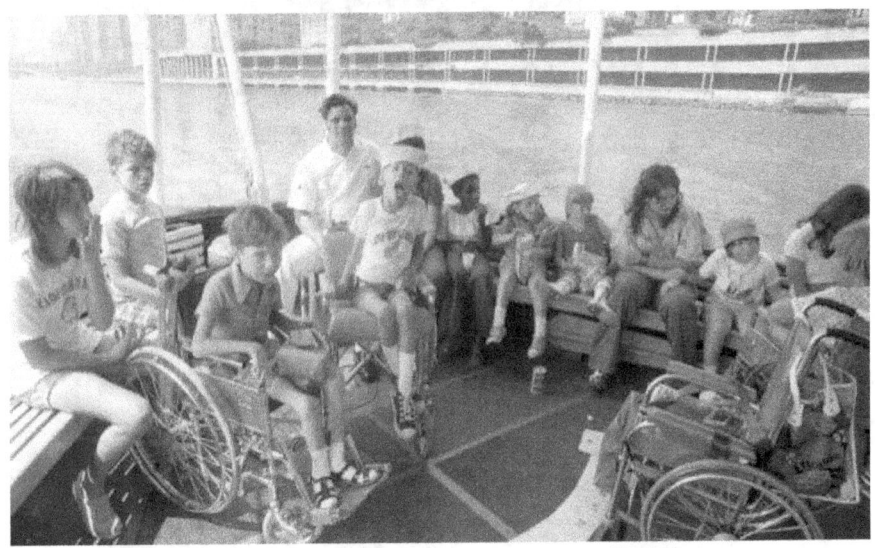

A Coast Guard Outing For Disabled Children.

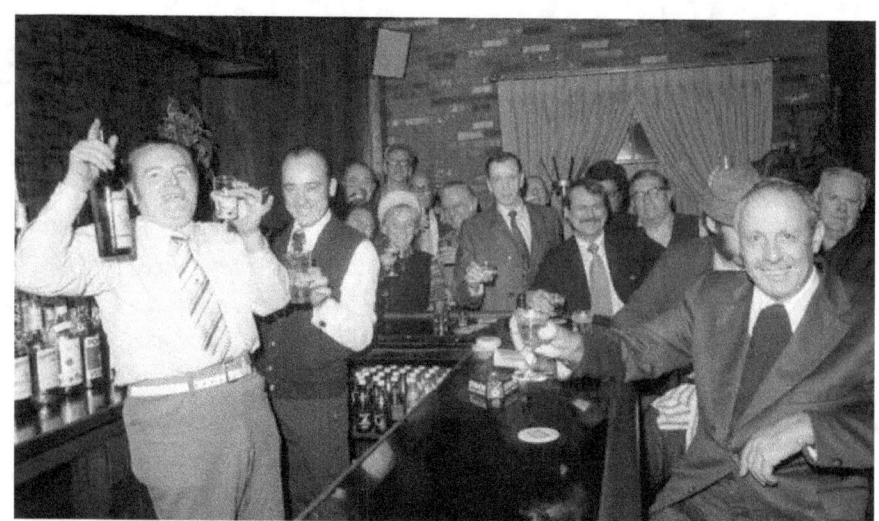

The End Of A Liquor Delivery Strike In A Queens Tavern!

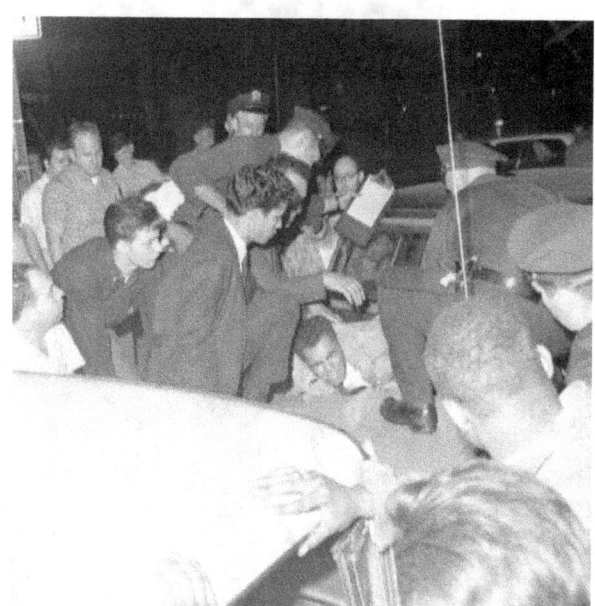

Car Crash Victim Being Rescued

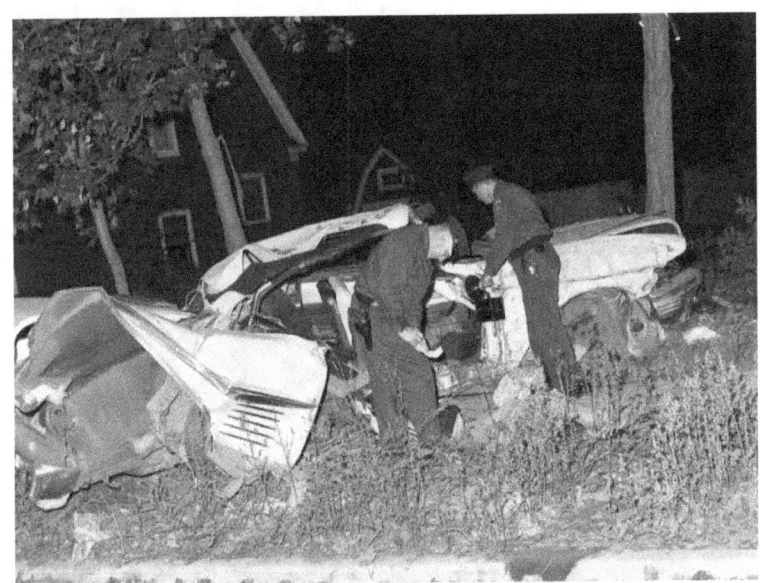
Two Died In This Car Accident!

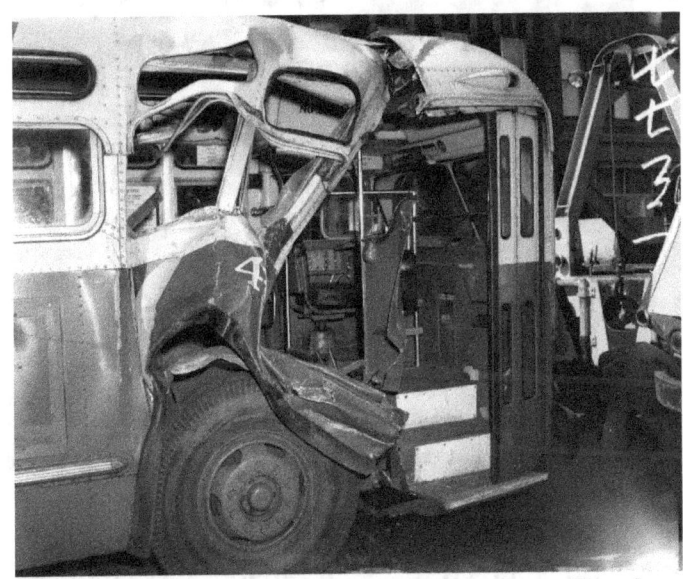
This Brooklyn Bus Rammed a Beverage Truck.

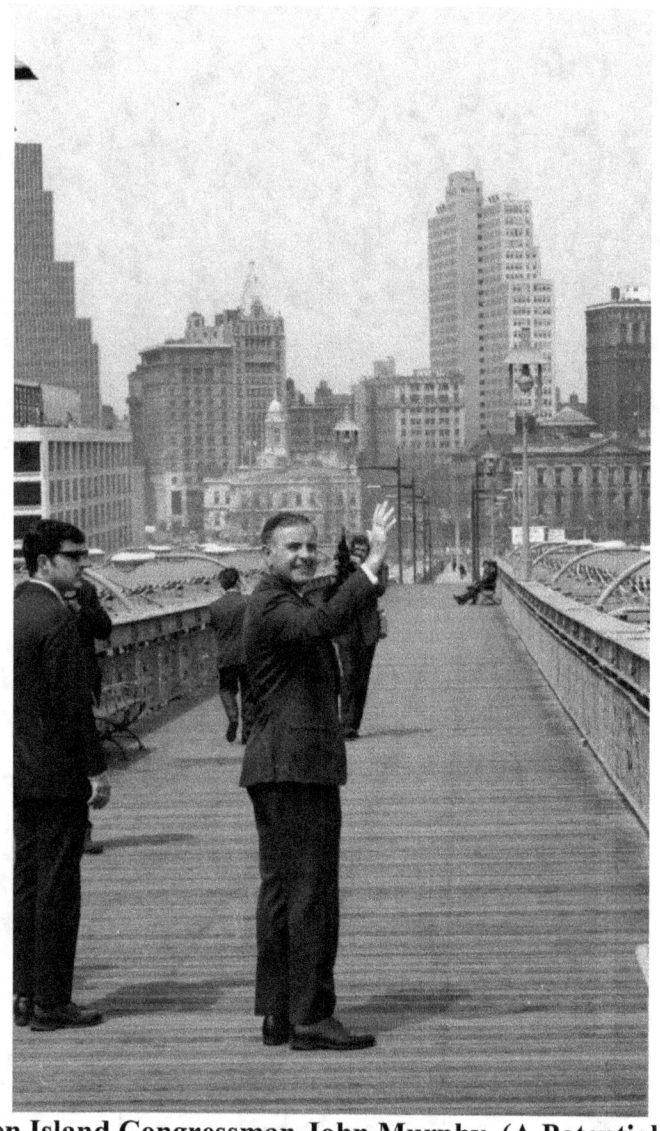

Staten Island Congressman John Murphy, (A Potential V.P. Nominee, Until Derailed in ABSCAM Scandal) waves on the Brooklyn Bridge.

As I get older, more memories flood back. These are stories that did not appear in my first book.

***

MEETING MOTHER TERESA

While waiting for my daughter to arrive on a flight from New Orleans at New York's LaGuardia Airport in July of 1995, I looked to my left as passengers were leaving from another flight. I noticed a group of nuns in white-and-blue habits. Low and behold, Mother Teresa was in the lead! I jumped from my seat and stood directly in front of the tiny nun, extending my right hand and said, "Mother Teresa." She stopped, clasped my hand with both of hers, looked directly into my eyes and said, "Pray, Pray." She then reached into a tiny cloth purse, took out a prayer card, signed her name, handed it to me and was off in a flash with her nuns in tow. I didn't take a picture, but those ten seconds was an experience that I shall never forget. Holding hands with a Saint left me with an indelible mark.

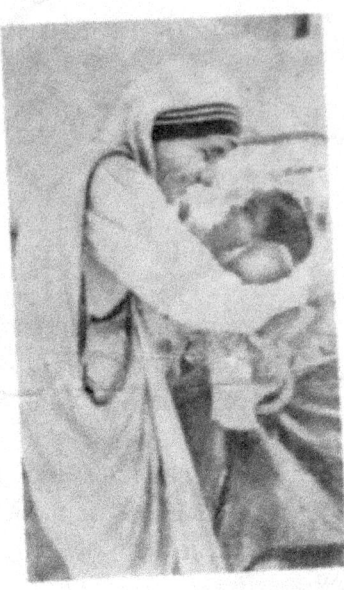

LOVE TO PRAY — feel often during the day the need for prayer and take trouble to pray. Prayer enlarges the heart until it is capable of containing God's gift of Himself. Ask and seek, and your heart will grow big enough to receive Him and keep Him as your own.

In union with all the Masses being offered throughout the Catholic world, I offer you my heart. Make it meek and humble like yours.

God bless you
M Teresa mc

WE ALL GOTTA EAT!

While working in Brooklyn, a detective friend of reporter Bill Travers paid us a visit with another man, who turned out to be his prisoner for some low-level crime. The detective had to wait for some paperwork to be filed in the "Seven-Eight" precinct, which was across the street from the Daily News office. We all headed down to Willie Henderson's, a bar and grill, on the corner of 6th Avenue and Dean Street. As this was the Wednesday before Thanksgiving, Willie was offering free delicious fresh turkey sandwiches to all patrons. Introductions were made while we ate at the bar. I thought Henderson would have a stroke when he found out one of his patrons was a prisoner, and not the detective's partner!

AN EMOTIONAL BUT SATISFYING TRIP

In March of 1979, I was assigned to make some photos of entertainment people departing from JFK airport to Amsterdam promoting tourism to the Big Apple. As New York was known. The campaign theme was *I LOVE NEW YORK*. The public relations man for National Airlines, the now defunct carrier for the trip, invited me to join them. Since my passport was at home, and I had no permission from my boss, I sadly had to turn him down.

No problem, he remarked. If you do receive permission, we have another flight leaving tomorrow night. So, then I asked my supervisor, Ed Peters, a wonderful man, if he would assign me to the Holland trip. "Tom, I couldn't send you to New Jersey," Ed replied. But he asked if I had accumulated any time off. I said yes, and he approved my request of four days off.

"Enjoy the trip," he added.

My wife had my bag packed the next evening when I shocked her by saying, "Pack you bag and grab your passport, you're going too," as I handed her a ticket I'd purchased earlier that day.

It was a great trip. I photographed the cast of "Grease" doing their show at a hotel in Amsterdam, then headed to the United Press International (UPI) office, developed my film and wired a couple of pix back to the Daily News in New York. The night photo editor, George Mattson, remarked to fellow photog Charlie Ruppmann that there had to be a mistake in the credit line, which had my name under the picture. No mistake, replied Charlie, Tom is in Amsterdam!

We toured Amsterdam's sites, and were emotionally overwhelmed when we went through the Anne Frank House. One can only imagine what went through the minds of those poor people, hearing jack-booted Gestapo thugs climbing the wooden staircase to arrest and send them off to extermination camps, just because they were Jews. Eight people hid for 761 days in a secret attic before an informant turned them in to the Nazis. My wife and I still have chills thinking about it.

On a happier note, we took a train to Rotterdam, then a bus to Volendam, as I wanted to photograph the famous Holland Windmills. It was a great site and my photo won first prize in the pictorial class of the New York Press Photographers Association (NYPPA) contest in 1979.

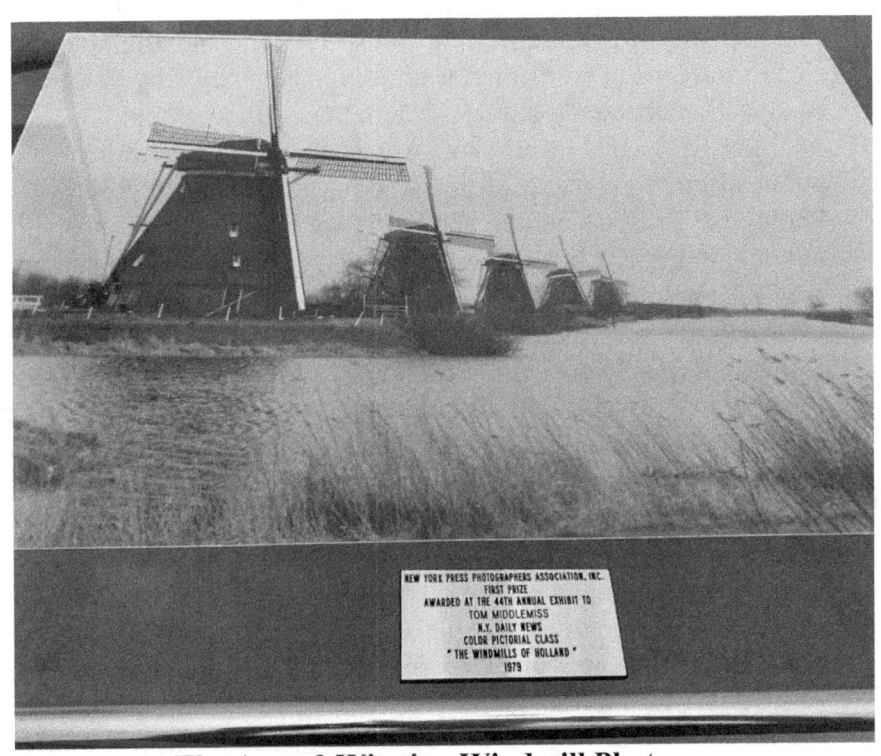

The Award-Winning Windmill Photo

A VERY MERRY CHRISTMAS

The New York Press Photographers Christmas party was, by far, the best in New York City.

Hosted by International Telephone & Telegraph (ITT) and held at the St. Regis Hotel on East 55th Street in Manhattan, nothing was spared in the way of food, drink and soft live music. The hotel oozed elegance from the moment you set foot inside the lobby to the beautifully decorated ballroom where the event was held.

Edward "Ned" Gerrity, who was in charge of government and public affairs ITT, was a great friend of the New York Press Photographers Association, and he showed it with the sponsorship of not only this party, but numerous contest categories in the annual NYPPA photo contest.

Another one of Ned's parties was the Brussels Boys Club event at the St. Regis. Named after a statue of a youngster urinating in a fountain in Brussels, Gerrity had a replica of the famed fountain, boy and all, in the ballroom. It was a raucous event with plenty a great food, drink and entertainment for some 200 guests, all from various news organizations in New York City.

At one particular party, Red Buttons was on stage telling his jokes when a chimpanzee came speeding in on a pair of roller skates, with his handler in tow. The place went wild as the chimp skated around the ballroom when George Mattson, the night Picture Assignment Editor at the Daily News stopped the chimp and offered the animal a highball glass of Grand Marnier Liqueur, followed with a bottle of Heineken (The Green Monster) for a chaser.

The chimp went crazy, screeching while skating as if he was possessed, trying to climb the drapes. Needless to say, the guests went wild with laughter and applause, except the handler, who had his hands full getting the creature under control.

Red Buttons, no longer the star of the evening declared, "I can't compete with the chimp, I'm out of here" and left. It was truly an evening to remember.

TAKING THE STUDENTS TO THE COURTHOUSE

Ed Kirkman, a reporter friend with the Daily News, thought it would be a good idea if I could land a gig teaching photojournalism at St. John's University, my Queens alma mater. Ed was an adjunct journalism professor at the university and recommended me to the Chairman of the Department. I was interviewed and approved for the position, a three-hour morning class once a week.

This was a new experience, teaching 18 and 19-year-old students what press photography was all about. My first class almost proved to be a disaster. After speaking to the class for what I thought was about 45 minutes, I looked at my watch and realized only 15 minutes had passed. I got through it OK by answering loads of questions.

Halfway through the class, I gave them a coffee break. Before they left, I called on one young man to remove his baseball type hat in class. "There is no St. John's requirement that I remove my hat," he said. "You are correct," I replied. "That's my requirement."

When he returned after the break, the hat was removed, but his hair was down to his waist. I didn't say a word. Surprisingly, I never saw him again.

I decided that field trips would be most beneficial to my students, so I had them meet me at places where they would experience what I went through in my career, and what they might encounter should they take up the profession.

One such trip was to the Queens County Court House in Kew Gardens. We assembled in the lobby and proceeded to a courtroom where people were arraigned. This is where anyone who is arrested the night before is brought before a judge, pleads guilty or not guilty, and bail is set. The defendant either makes bail or is remanded to jail for a hearing at a later date.

My 10 students and I took seats, and I recognized the judge as a woman who was a friend of my wife's. After a few minutes, a court officer approached me and said, "The judge wants to see you."

I approached the bench, introduced myself as Marianne's husband. She smiled broadly and directed the court officer to place my students and I behind her on the bench as she meted out justice. To this day, I find it hard to believe what she did. It was a wonderful experience, not only for me, but the whole class.

Field trips were great. I could take the students to places they might never see: the New York Daily News City room; our studio, home to 54 staff photographers; the Associated Press. And even the control tower at JFK Airport, where they could watch, listen and photograph controllers as they guided aircraft in and out of one the world's busiest airports.

One of my former students, Kevin Coughlin, went on to become a Pulitzer Prize-sharing journalist, writer, governmental photographer, pilot and current executive photographer to New York's Governor Andrew Cuomo.

Way to go Kevin, I am very proud of you.

A REAL HERO

When my wife and I moved to Naples in 2004, I was looking for something to do in the newspaper field and went to work for the Naples Sun Times, a free weekly publication. It was a great way to learn about the city and meet lots of people. The editor of the paper, Lawrence De Maria (also the editor of this book), suggested we feature members of the Greatest Generation, WW II heroes who saved the world.

I interviewed and photographed many of those men, but one who really stood out in my mind was Everett Short, a Frenchburg, Kentucky native who joined the United States Marine Corps on his 17th birthday, September 3, 1942. Short went on to fight at Guadalcanal, Bougainville, Guam and Iwo Jima. Iwo was one of the bloodiest battles in the history of the Corps. It suffered 26,000 casualties, 6,800 of whom were killed. The Japanese defenders lost 19,000 men in the battle.

Short was discharged on December 19, 1945, married and had four boys, two of whom went to West Point. The other two sons followed in their dad's footsteps and joined the Marines.

Short passed away on September 24, 2014.

I included this story to memorialize what men like Short and millions like him saved the world and ended the Holocaust.

The picture I made of him says it all…the uniform, our beloved flag and last but not least, a face which speaks nothing but integrity and patriotism.

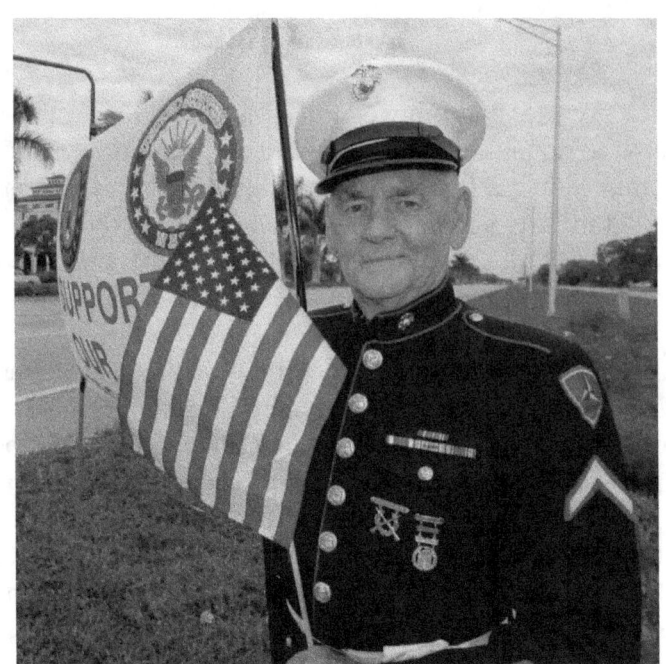

Everett Short, U.S.M.C.

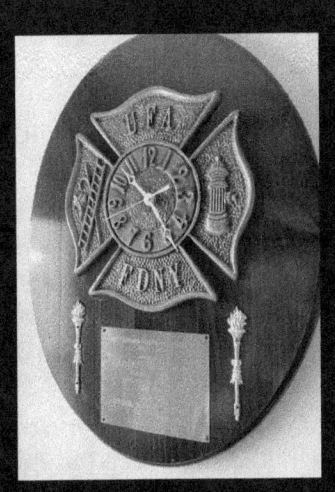 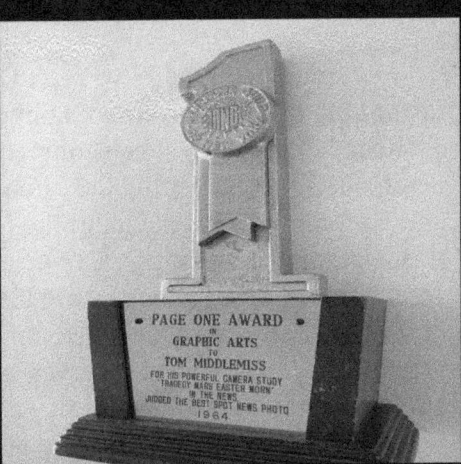

AWARDS AND HONORS

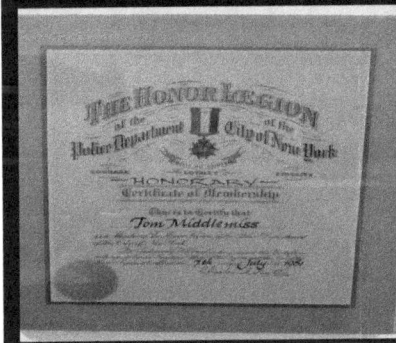 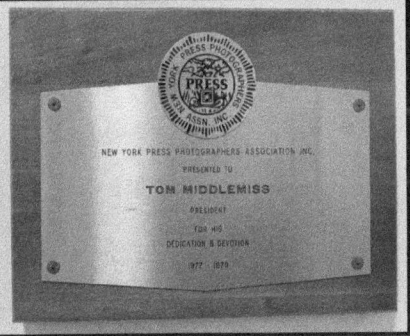

EPILOGUE

My tenure with the New York Daly News was exciting and rewarding. Each and every assignment was different, and many were challenges, especially when competing wire services and other newspapers were covering the same story.

Becoming the president of the New York Press Photographers Association, the oldest press association in North America, was a great honor. Its 220 members are the finest and best photojournalists in the business, who cooperated not only with each other, but, in certain situations, with rules given by those whom we were covering. In that regard, we were respected.

I salute my fellow members, and ask that they keep the spirit of our famed organization alive forever.

THE END
(For Now!)

EMAIL: tom@eventpixer.com

WEBSITE: www.eventpixer.com

www.ingramcontent.com/pod-product-compliance
Lightning Source LLC
Chambersburg PA
CBHW070456220526
45466CB00004B/1847